SUBSIDIA MEDIAEVALIA

9

THE TRADITION OF MEDIEVAL LOGIC AND SPECULATIVE GRAMMAR

from Anselm to the End of the Seventeenth Century:

A Bibliography from 1836 Onwards

BY

E. J. ASHWORTH

PONTIFICAL INSTITUTE OF MEDIAEVAL STUDIES
TORONTO, CANADA
1978

ACKNOWLEDGMENT

This book has been published with the help of a grant from the Humanities Research Council of Canada, using funds provided by the Canada Council.

Canadian Cataloguing in Publication Data

Ashworth, Earline J., 1939-
  The tradition of medieval logic and speculative grammar from Anselm to the end of the seventeenth century

(Subsidia mediaevalia; 9 ISSN 0316-0769)

Includes index.
ISBN 0-88844-358-7

1. Logic, Medieval - Bibliography. I. Pontifical Institute of Mediaeval Studies.
II. Title.
III. Series.

Z7128.L7A85　　　　　　　　016.16　　　　　　　　C78-001027-2

© 1978 by
PONTIFICAL INSTITUTE OF MEDIAEVAL STUDIES
59 Queen's Park Crescent East
Toronto, Ontario, Canada M5S 2C4

PRINTED BY UNIVERSA, WETTEREN, BELGIUM

Contents

Preface VII

Part One.   ANSELM TO PAUL OF VENICE (items 1-632)   1
Part Two.   AFTER PAUL OF VENICE (items 633-879) 73

Index of Names 101
Index of Texts 105
Index of Translations 107
Index of Subjects 109

Preface

My main interest in drawing up this bibliography was to list all the books and articles which have to do with formal logic and semantics from the time of Anselm to the end of the seventeenth century. I see this area as including such topics as consequences, syllogistic, supposition theory, and speculative grammar, but as excluding such topics as the categories, the struggle between nominalism and realism, and pure grammar. It is not, of course, always easy to draw a line between works which are concerned with formal logic and semantics and works which are not so concerned, and inevitably my choice of borderline cases will seem too restrictive to some and too liberal to others. However, my hope is that I have not excluded any book or article which obviously falls into the area I have delimited.

I have used the phrase "the tradition of medieval logic" in the title in order to indicate that although I include the seventeenth century, I am not concerned with the contributions of modern philosophy. The work of men such as Pascal, Descartes, Arnauld, Leibniz and Locke carries us far indeed from medieval discussions of logic and semantics. Moreover, there is already such an extensive literature on these figures that to include them in my bibliography would completely change its character. On the other hand, I do include humanist logic and renaissance Aristotelianism, since they involve a reaction to the medieval tradition which can only properly be understood in the light of that tradition.

This is a bibliography of secondary works and of modern editions of early texts. Accordingly I have excluded those nineteenth century reprints of earlier works such as Aldrich's *Artis Logicae Compendium* which were produced merely as text books, and I have also excluded modern facsimile editions of early printed texts unless they are accompanied by substantial editorial material. In addition, I have omitted a list of the various editions of Milton's *Artis Logicae Plenior Institutio*, since printings of his complete works are both numerous and easily found. The earliest book I list is Victor Cousin's 1836 edition of Abelard, since this can properly be viewed as the starting point of modern scholarly work on medieval logicians.

I do not refer to short edited or translated passages in books of readings. I have included only the more lengthy book reviews, and only a few unpublished dissertations. I have not included biographical and general historical works unless they have some specific contribution to make to the history of logic. I have tried to include all relevant material published before 1977, but the listing of 1976 publications is inevitably incomplete, given the delays which so often occur in the printing of books and journals.

I have endeavoured to look at each item personally, and to include as much information as possible. In those cases where I have failed to locate an item, or have located it in a place where I could not conveniently see it, I have made a note of my failure. The reader should bear in mind that these entries may be quite inaccurate. Where I have only been able to see a copy of an article, I have added the note: "Journal not seen."

Works which deal with the period as a whole will be found in Part One.

Where an author has more than one book or article, the items are arranged chronologically.

Below each item I list the headings under which it is indexed and, where relevant, cross-references to reviews, discussions, translations and reprints. The ordering of the headings corresponds to the four indexes I have provided: (1) an index of names; (2) an index of texts; (3) an index of translations; (4) an index of subjects. Only substantial texts and translations are indexed. In the few cases where a book review is not cross-referenced, the reason is that only the review contains material relevant to my purposes. It is my hope that these indexes, which are based on my knowledge of a work's contents rather than its title alone, will prove one of the most valuable aspects of my bibliography.

Readers who wish to find articles dealing with related fields or published after 1976 are recommended to consult two bibliographical sources in particular. They are:

1. *Répertoire Bibliographique de la Philosophie*. Publié par l'Institut supérieur de philosophie de l'Université catholique de Louvain.

2. *The Philosopher's Index.* An International Index to Philosophical Periodicals.

Readers who wish to remedy the omissions I describe in my first three paragraphs are also recommended to consult the following:

Risse, Wilhelm. *Bibliographia Logica.* Band II. *1801-1969.* Hildesheim-New York: Georg Olms Verlag, 1973.

Risse's work is far more comprehensive than my own, since he includes not only formal logic, but what might be described as the logic of ideas. On the other hand, his bibliography is arranged chronologically rather than alphabetically; and inevitably, given the scope of his work, he does not give full publication details and his indexes are minimal. Volume II contains only books, and it is to be hoped that the volume listing journal articles will appear before too long.

I owe a great debt of gratitude to those people who went through an earlier version of this bibliography and provided me with a large number of extra references. In particular I would like to thank William McMahon, Jan Pinborg, Charles Schmitt, and Paul Vincent Spade. I would also like to thank the editorial staff of the Pontifical Institute of Mediaeval Studies for their helpful advice on organization and presentation, the staff of Inter-Library Loan at the University of Waterloo for their unfailing help, and the Canada Council for various grants which have enabled me to work in British libraries. Finally, I should like to thank the Humanities Research Council of Canada for aiding the publication of this book.

August, 1977   E. J. Ashworth
University of Waterloo

Part One

Anselm to Paul of Venice

1. Abelard, Peter. *Peter Abaelards Philosophische Schriften. I. Die Logica 'Ingredientibus'. 1. Die Glossen zu Porphyrius.* Edited by B. Geyer. *Beiträge zur Geschichte der Philosophie des Mittelalters. Texte und Untersuchungen.* Band 21. Heft 1. Münster i.W.: Aschendorff, 1919.
   [Abelard. Text. Porphyry commentary.]

2. ———. *Peter Abaelards Philosophische Schriften. I. Die Logica 'Ingredientibus'. 2. Die Glossen zu den Kategorien.* Edited by B. Geyer. *Beiträge zur Geschichte der Philosophie des Mittelalters. Texte und Untersuchungen.* Band 21. Heft 2. Münster i.W.: Aschendorff, 1921.
   [Abelard. Text. Aristotle commentary.]

3. ———. *Peter Abaelards Philosophische Schriften. I. Die Logica 'Ingredientibus'. 2. Die Glossen zu ΠΕΡΙ ΕΡΜΗΝΕΙΑΣ.* Edited by B. Geyer. *Beiträge zur Geschichte der Philosophie des Mittelalters. Texte und Untersuchungen.* Band 21. Heft 3. Münster i.W.: Aschendorff, 1927.
   [Abelard. Text. Aristotle commentary.]

4. ———. *Peter Abaelards Philosophische Schriften. II. Die Logica 'Nostrorum Petitioni Sociorum'. Die Glossen zu Porphyrius.* Edited by B. Geyer. *Beiträge zur Geschichte der Philosophie des Mittelalters. Texte und Untersuchungen.* Band 21. Heft 4. Münster i.W.: Aschendorff, 1933.
   [Abelard. Text. Porphyry commentary.]

5. ———. Pietro Abelardo. *Scritti filosofici. Editio super Porphyrium. Glossae in Categorias. Editio super Aristotelem De Interpretatione. De divisionibus. Super Topica glossae.* Editi per la prima volta da Mario Dal Pra. Roma-Milano: Fratelli Bocca Editori, 1954.
   [Abelard. Text. Aristotle commentary.]

6. ———. Petrus Abaelardus. *Dialectica. First complete edition of the Parisian manuscript*, with an introduction by L. M. de Rijk. Assen: Van Gorcum, 1956. 2nd, revised edition. Assen: Van Gorcum, 1970.
[Abelard. Text.]

7. ———. Pietro Abelardo. *Scritti di Logica*, editi da Mario dal Pra. Firenze: La Nuova Italia Editrice, 1969.
[Abelard. Text.]

8. Abranches, Cassiano. "Pedro Hispano e as 'Summulae Logicales'." *Revista Portuguesa de Filosofia* 8 (1952): 243-259.
[Not seen.]
[Peter of Spain.]
———. See also Part Two: 634.

9. Adams, Marilyn McCord. "Did Ockham Know of Material and Strict Implication? A Reconsideration." *Franciscan Studies* 33 (1973): 5-37.
[Ockham. Implication.]

10. ———. "What does Ockham mean by 'Supposition'?" *Notre Dame Journal of Formal Logic* 17 (1976): 375-391.
[Ockham. Supposition.]

11. Albert the Great. Albertus Magnus. *Opera Omnia ... cura ac labore Augusti Borgnet. Volumen Primum. Logicae Prima Pars. Volumen Secundum. Logicae Secunda Pars.* Parisiis: apud Ludovicum Vivès, Bibliopolam Editorem, 1890.
[Albert the Great. Text.]

12. Alessio, Franco. "Prospettive e Problemi della Storia della Logica Medievale." In *Atti del Convegno di Storia della Logica (Parma 8-10 Ottobre 1972)*, pp. 37-59. Padova: Liviana Editrice, 1974.
[Logic, history of.]

13. Ammonius. *Commentaire sur le Peri Hermeneias d'Aristote. Traduction de Guillaume de Moerbeke. Édition critique et étude sur l'utilisation du commentaire dans l'œuvre de Saint Thomas* par G. Verbeke. *Corpus latinum commentariorum in Aristotelem Graecorum* II. Louvain, Paris: Publications Universitaires de Louvain, Éditions Béatrice-Nauwelaerts, 1961.
[Thomas Aquinas. William of Moerbeke. Ammonius: Latin.]

14. Andrés, Teodoro de. "La significación 'representativa' en Guillermo de Ockham." *Pensamiento* 24 (1968): 375-381.
    [Ockham. Signification.]

15. ———. *El nominalismo de Guillermo de Ockham como filosofía del lenguaje.* Madrid: Editorial Gredos, S.A., 1969.
    [Ockham. Language. Nominalism.]

16. Angelelli, Ignacio. *Studies on Gottlob Frege and Traditional Philosophy.* Dordrecht, Holland: D. Reidel Publishing Company, 1967.
    [Intentions. Predication.]

17. ———. [Review of] Jan Pinborg. *Logik und Semantik im Mittelalter. Ein Ueberblick.* In *Annals of Science* 32 (1975): 518.
    [Review of 417.]
    ———. See also Part Two: 635.

18. Apel, Karl Otto. *Die Idee der Sprache in der Tradition des Humanismus von Dante bis Vico. Archiv für Begriffsgeschichte* 8. Bonn: H. Bouvier u. Co., 1963.
    [Dante. Humanism. Language.]

19. Aristotle. *Aristoteles Latinus.* I: 1-5. *Categoriae vel Praedicamenta. Translatio Boethii - Editio Composita. Translatio Guillelmi de Moerbeka Lemmata e Simplicii Commentario Decerpta Pseudo-Augustini Paraphrasis Themistiana.* Edidit Laurentius Minio-Paluello. Bruges-Paris: Desclée de Brouwer, 1961.
    [William of Moerbeke. Text. Aristotle: Latin.]

20. ———. *Aristotle: On Interpretation. Commentary by St. Thomas and Cajetan (Peri Hermeneias).* Translated from the Latin with an Introduction by Jean J. Oesterle. Milwaukee, Wisc.: Marquette University Press, 1962.
    [Thomas Aquinas. Cajetan, Thomas de Vio. Translation. Aristotle commentary.]

21. ———. *Aristoteles Latinus.* III: 1-4. *Analytica Priora. Translatio Boethii (Recensiones Duae) Translatio Anonyma Pseudo-Philoponi Aliorumque Scholia. Specimina Translationum Recentiorum.* Edidit Laurentius Minio-Paluello. Bruges-Paris: Desclée de Brouwer, 1962.
    [Text. Aristotle: Latin.]

22. ———. *Aristoteles Latinus.* II: 1-2. *De Interpretatione vel Periermenias. Translatio Boethii. Specimina Translationum Recentiorum.*

Edidit Laurentius Minio-Paluello. *Translatio Guillermi de Moerbeka.* Edidit Gerardus Verbeke. Revisit L. Minio-Paluello. Bruges-Paris: Desclée de Brouwer, 1965.
[William of Moerbeke. Text. Aristotle: Latin.]

23. ———. *Aristoteles Latinus.* I: 6-7. *Categoriarum Supplementa. Porphyrii Isagoge. Translatio Boethii et Anonymi Fragmentum vulgo vocatum 'Liber Sex Principiorum' Accedunt Isagoges Fragmenta M. Victorino Interprete et Specimina Translationum Recentiorum Categoriarum.* Edidit Laurentius Minio-Paluello adiuvante Bernardo G. Dod. Bruges-Paris: Desclée de Brouwer, 1966.
[Text. Aristotle: Latin. Porphyry: Latin.]

24. ———. *Aristoteles Latinus.* IV: 1-4. 2 et 3 editio altera. *Analytica Posteriora. Translationes Iacobi, Anonymi sive 'Ioannis', Gerardi et Recensio Guillelmi de Moerbeka.* Ediderunt Laurentius Minio-Paluello et Bernardus G. Dod. Bruges-Paris: Desclée de Brouwer, 1968.
[William of Moerbeke. Text. Aristotle: Latin.]

25. ———. *Aristoteles Latinus.* V: 1-3. *Topica. Translatio Boethii. Fragmentum Recensionis Alterius, et Translatio Anonyma.* Edidit Laurentius Minio-Paluello. Adiuvante Bernardo G. Dod. Bruges-Paris: Desclée de Brouwer, 1969.
[Text. Aristotle: Latin.]

26. ———. *Aristoteles Latinus.* VI: 1-3. *De Sophisticis Elenchis. Translatio Boethii. Fragmenta Translationis Iacobi, et Recensio Guillelmi de Moerbeke.* Edidit Bernardus G. Dod. Bruxelles: Desclée de Brouwer, Leiden: E. J. Brill, 1975.
[William of Moerbeke. Text. Aristotle: Latin.]

27. Arnold, Erwin. "*Zur Geschichte der Suppositionstheorie.* 'Die Würzeln des modernen europäischen Subjektivismus'." *Symposion. Jahrbuch für Philosophie* 3 (1952): 1-134.
[Supposition.]

28. Aspelin, Gunnar. "John of Salisbury's *Metalogicon.* A Study in Mediaeval Humanism." *Bulletin de la Société royale des lettres de Lund* (1951-1952): 19-37. [Journal not seen.]
[John of Salisbury.]

29. Auer-Bonn, Johann. "Die aristotelische Logik in der Trinitätslehre der Spätscholastik. Bemerkungen zu einer Quaestio des Johannes Wuel de Pruck. Wien 1422." In *Theologie in Geschichte und Gegen-*

wart. Michael Schmaus zum sechzigsten Geburtstag dargebracht von seinen Freunden und Schülern herausgegeben von Johann Auer und Hermann Volk, pp. 457-496. München: Karl Zink, 1957.
[Johannes Wuel. Text. Paralogisms. Theology.]

30. Bacon, Roger. *Summa de Sophismatibus et Distinctionibus* in *Opera hactenus inedita Rogeri Baconi* .... Edidit Robert Steele, Fasc. 14. Oxonii, 1937.
[Bacon, Roger. Text.]

31. ———. *Summa Gramatica Magistri Rogeri Bacon necnon Sumule Dialectices Magistri Rogeri Bacon Nunc Primum Edidit Robert Steele.* In *Opera hactenus inedita Rogeri Baconi,* Fasc. 15. Oxonii, 1940.
[Bacon, Roger. Text.]

32. Baeumker, Clemens. *Die Impossibilia des Siger von Brabant. Beiträge zur Geschichte der Philosophie des Mittelalters. Texte und Untersuchungen.* Band 2. Heft 6. Münster, 1898.
[Siger of Brabant. Text.]

33. Barth, Else Margarete. *De Logica van de Lidwoorden in de traditionele Filosofie.* Leiden: Universitaire Pers, 1971.
[Copula. Definite article. Supposition.]
[Translation: 34.]

34. ———. *The Logic of the Articles in Traditional Philosophy. A Contribution to the Study of Conceptual Structures.* Translated from the Dutch by E. M. Barth and T. C. Potts. Synthèse Historical Library 10. Dordrecht, Holland and Boston, U.S.A.: D. Reidel Publishing Company, 1974.
[Copula. Definite article. Supposition.]
[Translation of 33.]

35. Barth, Timotheus. "Die Summa Logicae des Wilhelm Ockham und der Traktat de puritate artis logicae des Walter Burleigh in zwei Handschriften der Kommunalbibliothek von Treviso." *Franziskanische Studien* 37 (1955): 411-416.
[Burleigh. Ockham.]

36. Baudry, Léon. "Le Texte de la *Summa Totius Logicae.*" *Mediaeval Studies* 9 (1947): 301-304.
[Ockham.]
———. See also Part Two: 660.

37. Bazán, Bernardo. Siger de Brabant. *Écrits de logique, de morale et de physique*. Philosophes médiévaux 14. Louvain: Publications universitaires, Paris: Éditions Béatrice Nauwelaerts, 1974.
[Siger of Brabant. Text.]
38. Beckmann, Jan P. [Review of] Peter of Spain (Petrus Hispanus Portugalensis) *Tractatus called afterward Summule Logicales*. First Critical Edition from the manuscripts with an Introduction by L. M. de Rijk. In *Archiv für Geschichte der Philosophie* 58 (1976): 70-72.
[Review of 403.]
39. Bendiek, Johannes. "Die Lehre von den Konsequenzen bei Pseudo-Scotus." *Franziskanische Studien* 34 (1952): 205-234.
[Pseudo-Scotus. Consequences.]
40. [Beonio-Brocchieri] Fumagalli, Maria Teresa. "Note sulla logica di Abelardo. I. La concezione abelardiana della logica." *Rivista critica di storia della filosofia* 13 (1958): 12-26.
[Abelard. Logic, concept of.]
41. ———. "Note sulla logica di Abelardo. II. Il problema del significato." *Rivista critica di storia della filosofia* 13 (1958): 280-290.
[Abelard. Meaning. Reference.]
42. ———. "Note sulla logica di Abelardo. III. Il significato dei nomi universali." *Rivista critica di storia della filosofia* 14 (1959): 3-27.
[Abelard. Universals.]
43. ———. "Note sulla logica di Abelardo. IV. Il significato della 'propositio'." *Rivista critica di storia della filosofia* 15 (1960): 14-21.
[Abelard. Significate of the proposition.]
44. ———. "Note sulla logica di Abelardo. (V-VI) [V. L'*Argumentatio*'. VI. Abaelardiana inedita.]" *Rivista critica di storia della filosofia* 18 (1963): 131-146.
[Abelard. Consequences.]
45. Beonio-Brocchieri Fumagalli, Maria Teresa. *La logica di Abelardo*. Firenze: La Nuova Italia Editrice, 1964. Second edition, 1969.
[Abelard.]
[Translation: 46.]
46. ———. *The Logic of Abelard*. Synthèse Historical Library 1. Dordrecht, Holland: D. Reidel Publishing Company, 1969.
[Abelard.]
[Translation of 45.]

47. ——. "La relation entre logique, physique et théologie chez Abélard." In *Peter Abelard. Proceedings of the International Conference Louvain May 10-12 1971* edited by E. M. Buytaert, pp. 153-162. Leuven: University Press, The Hague: Martinus Nijhoff, 1974.
[Abelard.]

48. Bird, Otto, "The Logical Interest of the Topics as seen in Abelard." *The Modern Schoolman* 37 (1959-1960): 53-57.
[Abelard. Topics.]
[Review: 597.]

49. ——. "The Formalizing of the Topics in Mediaeval Logic." *Notre Dame Journal of Formal Logic* 1 (1960): 138-149.
[Abelard. Consequences. Topics.]
[Review: 597.]

50. ——. "The Re-Discovery of the Topics. Professor Toulmin's Inference-Warrants." *Mind* 70 (1961): 534-539.
[Topics.]
[Review: 597.]

51. ——. "Topic and Consequence in Ockham's Logic." *Notre Dame Journal of Formal Logic* 2 (1961): 65-78.
[Ockham. Consequences. Topics.]
[Review: 597.]

52. ——. "The Tradition of the Logical Topics: Aristotle to Ockham." *Journal of the History of Ideas* 23 (1962): 307-323.
[Topics.]

53. ——. "The History of Logic." *The Review of Metaphysics* 16 (1962-1963): 491-502.
[Discussion of 62 and 267.]

54. Blarer, Joseph. "Alberti Magni 'De antecedentibus ad logicam' recensuit Joseph Blarer." *Teoresi* 9 (1954): 177-242. [Not seen.]
[Albert the Great. Text.]

55. Bocheński, Innocentius Maria. "Notes historiques sur les propositions modales." *Revue des sciences philosophiques et théologiques* 26 (1937): 673-692.
[Modal logic.]

56. ——. "De consequentiis scholasticorum earumque origine." *Angelicum* 15 (1938): 92-109.
[Consequences.]

57. ———. *Z historii logiki zdán modalnych.* Lwów: Wydawnictwo oo. Dominikanów, 1938.
   [Modal logic.]

58. ———. "Sancti Thomae Aquinatis de modalibus opusculum et doctrina." *Angelicum* 17 (1940): 180-218.
   [Thomas Aquinas. Text. Modal logic.]

59. ———. "Communications sur la logique médiévale." *The Journal of Symbolic Logic* 20 (1955): 90-91.
   [Implication. Insolubilia. Syllogistic.]

60. ———. "Scholastic and Aristotelian Logic." *Proceedings of the American Catholic Philosophical Association* 30 (1956): 112-117.
   [Logic, history of.]

61. ———. *Formale Logik.* Freiburg-München: Verlag Karl Alber, 1956.
   [Logic, history of.]
   [Translation: 62.]

62. ———. *A History of Formal Logic*, translated and edited by Ivo Thomas. Notre Dame, Ind.: University of Notre Dame Press, 1961.
   [Logic, history of.]
   [Translation of 61.]
   [Discussion: 53.]

63. ———. "Formalization of a Scholastic Solution of the Paradox of the 'Liar'." In *Logico-Philosophical Studies*, edited by Albert Menne, pp. 64-66. Dordrecht: D. Reidel Publishing Company, 1962.
   [Paul of Venice. Insolubilia.]
   ———. See also Part Two: 663.

64. Boehner, Philotheus. "Ein Gedicht auf die Logik Ockhams." *Franziskanische Studien* 26 (1939): 78-85.
   [Ockham.]

65. ———. "Zur Echtheit der Summa Logicae Ockhams." *Franziskanische Studien* 26 (1939): 190-193.
   [Ockham.]
   [Reprinted: 79.]

66. ———. "Ockham's *Tractatus de Praedestinatione et de Praescientia Dei et de Futuris Contingentibus* and Its Main Problems." *Proceedings of the American Catholic Philosophical Association* 16 (1941): 177-192.
   [Ockham. Future contingents.]
   [Reprinted: 79.]

67. ——. "The *Centiloquium* attributed to Ockham." *Franciscan Studies* 1, No. 1 (1941): 58-72. Continued: Ibid., 1, No. 2 (1941): 35-54; Ibid., 1, No. 3 (1941): 62-70; Ibid., 2 (1942): 49-60; Ibid., 2 (1942): 146-157; Ibid., 2 (1942): 251-301.
[Ockham. Text.]

68. ——. "The Medieval Crisis of Logic and the Author of the *Centiloquium* attributed to Ockham." *Franciscan Studies* 4 (1944): 151-170.
[Ockham.]
[Reprinted: 79.]

69. ——. "Ockham's Theory of Truth." *Franciscan Studies* 5 (1945): 138-161.
[Ockham. Truth.]
[Reprinted: 79.]

70. ——. "Ockham's Theory of Signification." *Franciscan Studies* 6 (1946): 143-170.
[Ockham. Signification.]
[Reprinted: 79.]

71. ——. "Ockham's Theory of Supposition and the Notion of Truth." *Franciscan Studies* 6 (1946): 261-292.
[Ockham. Supposition. Truth.]
[Reprinted: 79.]

72. ——. "A First Redaction of the *Expositio Aurea* of Ockham." *Franciscan Studies* 8 (1948): 69-76.
[Ockham.]
[Discussion of 308.]
[Reprinted: 79.]

73. ——. "Bemerkungen zur Geschichte der De Morganschen Gesetze in der Scholastik." *Archiv für Philosophie* 4 (1951): 113-146.
[Propositional logic.]

74. ——. "Three Sums of Logic attributed to William Ockham." *Franciscan Studies* 11 (1951): 173-193.
[Ockham.]
[Reprinted: 79.]

75. ——. "Does Ockham Know of Material Implication?" *Franciscan Studies* (1951) *St. Bonaventure University Commemorative Volume*, pp. 203-230.

[Ockham. Implication.]
[Reprinted: 79.]

76. ——. *Medieval Logic. An Outline of Its Development from 1250 to c. 1400.* Manchester: Manchester University Press, 1952.
[Logic, history of.]
[Discussion: 161.]

77. ——. "The Hypothetical First Redaction of Ockham's *Expositio Aurea.*" *Franciscan Studies* 14 (1954): 374-386.
[Ockham.]
[Reprinted: 79.]

78. ——. "A Medieval Theory of Supposition." *Franciscan Studies* 18 (1958): 240-289.
[Supposition.]

79. *Collected Articles on Ockham.* Edited by Eligius M. Buytaert. St. Bonaventure, N.Y., Louvain, Paderborn: The Franciscan Institute, 1958.
[Ockham.]
[Reprints of 65, 66, 68, 69, 70, 71, 72, 74, 75, 77.]

80. Boethius of Dacia. *Boethii Daci Opera. Modi Significandi sive Quaestiones super Priscianum Maiorem.* Nunc primum ediderunt Joannes Pinborg et Henricus Roos. Corpus Philosophorum Danicorum Medii Aevi 4. Hauniae: G. E. C. Gad, 1969.
[Boethius of Dacia. Text. Priscian commentary.]

81. ——. *Boethii Daci Opera. Topica-Opuscula.* Voluminis 6 Pars 1. *Quaestiones super Librum Topicorum.* Nunc primum ediderunt Nicolaus Georgius Green-Pedersen et Joannes Pinborg. Schedis usi Alfredi Otto. Hauniae: G. E. C. Gad, 1976.
[Boethius of Dacia. Text. Aristotle commentary.]

82. Boh, Ivan. "A Study in Burleigh: *Tractatus de regulis generalibus consequentiarum.*" *Notre Dame Journal of Formal Logic* 3 (1962): 83-101.
[Burleigh. Consequences.]

83. ——. "Walter Burleigh's Hypothetical Syllogistic." *Notre Dame Journal of Formal Logic* 4 (1963): 241-269.
[Burleigh. Consequences.]

84. ——. "Burleigh on Conditional Hypothetical Propositions." *Franciscan Studies* 23 (1963): 4-67.
[Burleigh. Text. Translation.]

85. ——. "An Examination of Ockham's Aretetic Logic." *Archiv für Geschichte der Philosophie* 45 (1963): 259-268.
    [Ockham. Aretetic logic.]
    [Review: 598.]

86. ——. "An Examination of Some Proofs in Burleigh's Propositional Logic." *The New Scholasticism* 38 (1964): 44-60.
    [Burleigh. Propositional logic.]
    ——. See also Part Two: 664-667.

87. Bos, E. P. "John Buridan and Marsilius of Inghen on Consequences." In *The Logic of John Buridan*, edited by Jan Pinborg, pp. 61-69. *Opuscula Graecolatina* (Supplementa Musei Tusculani), vol. 9. Copenhagen: Museum Tusculanum, 1976.
    [Buridan. Marsilius of Inghen. Consequences.]

88. Bottin, Francesco. "L"Opinio de insolubilibus' di Richard Kilmyngton." *Rivista critica di storia della filosofia* 28 (1973): 408-421.
    [Kilmington. Insolubilia.]

89. ——. "Analisi linguistica e fisica aristotelica nei 'Sophysmata' di Richard Kilmyngton." In *Filosofia e Politica e altri saggi*, a cura di C. Giacon, pp. 125-145. Padova: Editrice Antenore, 1973.
    [Kilmington. Sophisms.]

90. ——. "Un testo fondamentale nell'ambito della 'nuova fisica' di Oxford: i Sophismata di Richard Kilmington." In *Miscellanea Mediaevalia 9. Antiqui und Moderni. Traditionsbewusstsein und Fortschrittsbewusstsein im späten Mittelalter*, edited by A. Zimmermann, pp. 201-205. Berlin, New York: Walter de Gruyter, 1974.
    [Kilmington. Sophisms.]

91. ——. "Ruolo degli 'insolubilia' nella logica medievale." *Studia Mediewistyczne* 16 (1975): 15-37.
    [Insolubilia.]

92. ——. "Per una definizione di 'consequentia'." In *Logica e semantica ed altri saggi*, a cura di Carlo Giacon, pp. 17-36. Padova: Editrice Antenore, 1975.
    [Consequences.]

93. ——. *Le antinomie semantiche nella logica medievale*. Padova: Editrice Antenore, 1976.
    [Insolubilia.]
    ——. See also Part Two: 669-670.

94. Boyle, Leonard E. "Pierre Dubois and the *Summulae Logicales* of Peter of Spain." *Mediaeval Studies* 34 (1972): 468-470.
    [Peter of Spain.]

95. Braakhuis, H. A. G. "The second tract on insolubilia found in Paris, B.N. Lat. 16.617. An edition of the text with an analysis of its contents." *Vivarium* 5 (1967): 111-145.
    [Text. Insolubilia.]

96. Braswell, Bruce. "Godfrey of Fontaines' Abridgement of Boetius of Dacia's 'Quaestiones supra librum Topicorum Aristotelis'." *Mediaeval Studies* 26 (1964): 302-314.
    [Boethius of Dacia. Godfrey of Fontaines. Text (Godfrey of Fontaines).]

97. Brown, Sister Mary Anthony. "The Role of the *Tractatus de obligationibus* in Mediaeval Logic." *Franciscan Studies* 26 (1966): 26-55.
    [Obligations.]

98. Brown, Stephen F. "Walter Burleigh's Treatise *De Suppositionibus* and Its Influence on William of Ockham." *Franciscan Studies* 32 (1972): 15-64.
    [Burleigh. Ockham. Text (Burleigh). Supposition.]

99. ———. "Walter Burley's Middle Commentary on Aristotle's *Perihermeneias*." *Franciscan Studies* 33 (1973): 42-134.
    [Burleigh. Text. Aristotle commentary.]

100. ———. "Walter Burley's *Quaestiones in Librum Perihermeneias*." *Franciscan Studies* 34 (1974): 200-295.
    [Burleigh. Text. Aristotle commentary.]

101. ———. "Gerard Odon's 'De Suppositionibus'." *Franciscan Studies* 35 (1975): 5-44.
    [Odon. Text. Supposition.]

102. Buchanan, Scott. "An Introduction to the *De Modis Significandi* of Thomas of Erfurt." In *Philosophical Essays for Alfred North Whitehead* [by a group of his students], pp. 67-89. London, New York, Toronto: Longmans and Co., 1936.
    [Thomas of Erfurt. Modi significandi.]

103. Buridan, John. Buridano, Giovanni. "Tractatus de suppositionibus (Prima edizione a cura di Maria Elena Reina)." *Rivista critica di storia della filosofia* 12 (1957): 175-208, 323-352.
    [Buridan. Text. Supposition.]

104. ——. *Sophisms on Meaning and Truth.* Translated and with an introduction by T. K. Scott. New York: Appleton Century Crofts, 1966.
[Buridan. Translation. Insolubilia. Sophisms.]
[Reviews: 266, 452.]

105. Burleigh, Walter. *De Puritate Artis Logicae Tractatus Longior with a revised edition of the Tractatus Brevior.* Edited by Philotheus Boehner. St. Bonaventure, N.Y., Louvain, Paderborn: The Franciscan Institute, 1955.
[Burleigh. Text.]

106. Bursill-Hall, Geoffrey Leslie. "Mediaeval Grammatical Theories." *Canadian Journal of Linguistics* 9 (1963-1964): 40-54.
[Speculative grammar.]

107. ——. "Aspects of Modistic Grammar." In *Monograph Series on Languages and Linguistics (Report of the Seventeenth Annual Round Table Meeting on Linguistics and Language Studies)*, edited by Francis P. Dinneen, no. 19 (1966), pp. 133-148. Washington: Georgetown University Press, for the Institute of Languages and Linguistics, Georgetown University, 1966.
[Speculative grammar.]

108. ——. *Speculative Grammars of the Middle Ages. The Doctrine of Partes Orationis of the Modistae.* The Hague, Paris: Mouton, 1971.
[Speculative grammar.]
[Review: 260.]

109. ——. "Towards a History of Linguistics in the Middle Ages, 1100-1450." In *Studies in the History of Linguistics: Traditions and Paradigms*, edited by Dell Hymes, pp. 77-92. Bloomington, London: Indiana University Press, 1974.
[Speculative grammar.]

110. ——. "Some Notes on the Grammatical Theory of Boethius of Dacia." In *History of Linguistic Thought and Contemporary Linguistics*, edited by Herman Parret, pp. 164-188. Berlin, New York: Walter de Gruyter, 1976.
[Boethius of Dacia. Grammar.]

111. Buytaert, Eligius M. "The *Tractatus Logicae Minor* of Ockham." *Franciscan Studies* 24 (1964): 34-100.
[Ockham. Text.]

112. ———. "The *Elementarium Logicae* of Ockham." *Franciscan Studies* 25 (1965): 151-276.
    [Ockham. Text.]
    [Continued: 113.]

113. ———. "Guillelmi Ockham Elementarium logicae." *Franciscan Studies* 26 (1966): 66-173.
    [Ockham. Text.]
    [Continuation of 112.]

114. Capone Braga, Gaetano. "Della dialettica. Il Medio Evo." *Giornale di Metafisica* 9 (1954): 166-182. [Journal not seen.]
    [Abelard. Universals.]

115. Carruccio, Ettore. "La logica nel pensiero di Dante." *Physis* Anno 8 (1966): 233-246.
    [Dante. Peter of Spain. Aristotelianism: medieval.]

116. ———. "Teorema dello Pseudo-Scoto e Sue Applicazioni Metamatematiche." In *Atti del Convegno di Storia della Logica (Parma 8-10 Ottobre 1972)*, pp. 215-225. Padova: Liviana Editrice, 1974.
    [Pseudo-Scotus. Propositional logic.]

117. Chenu, Marie-Dominique. "Grammaire et Théologie au xiie et xiiie siècles." *Archives d'histoire doctrinale et littéraire du moyen âge* 10e et 11e années (1935-1936): 5-28.
    [Grammar. Theology.]

118. Chojnacki, Piotr. "L'essor de la logique au xiiie siècle." In *Arts libéraux et philosophie au moyen âge*, pp. 887-894. Montréal: Institut d'études médiévales, Paris: J. Vrin, 1969.
    [Logic, history of.]

119. Church, Alonzo. "The History of the Question of Existential Import of Categorical Propositions." In *Logic, Methodology and Philosophy of Science. Proceedings of the 1964 International Congress*, edited by Y Bar-Hillel, pp. 417-424. Amsterdam: North-Holland Publishing Company, 1965.
    [John of St. Thomas. Ockham. Existential import.]
    ———. See also Part Two: 675-676.

120. Clasen, Sophronius. "Henrici de Werla, O.F.M. Tractatus de Formalitatibus." *Franciscan Studies* 14 (1954): 310-322, 412-442.
    [Henry of Werla. Text.]

121. Cordoliani, A. "La *Logica* de Gerland de Besançon." *Revue du Moyen Age Latin* 5 (1949): 43-46.
[Gerland of Besançon.]

122. Courtenay, William J. "A Revised Text of Robert Holcot's Quodlibetal Dispute on Whether God is able to know more than He knows." *Archiv für Geschichte der Philosophie* 53 (1971): 1-21.
[Holkot. Text.]

123. Cousin, Victor. *Ouvrages inédits d'Abélard pour servir à l'histoire de la philosophie scolastique en France.* Paris: Imprimerie royale, 1836.
[Abelard. Text.]

124. Crombie, Alistair Cameron. "Scholastic Logic and the Experimental Method." *Archives internationales d'histoire des sciences* 1 (1947): 280-285.
[Duns Scotus. Ockham. Padua.]

125. Cunningham, F. A. "Speculative Grammar in St. Thomas Aquinas." *Laval Théologique et Philosophique* 17 (1961): 76-86.
[Thomas Aquinas. Speculative grammar.]

126. Dal Pra, Mario. "'Cogitatio vocum' et 'cogitatio rerum' nel pensiero di Anselmo." *Rivista critica di storia della filosofia* 9 (1954): 309-343.
[Anselm. Language. Meaning.]

127. ———. "Contributi filologici per la storia della filosofia II. Sulla dottrina della 'impositio prima et secunda'." *Rivista critica di storia della filosofia* 9 (1954): 390-399.
[Meaning.]

128. ———. "Gaunilone e il problema logico del linguaggio." *Rivista critica di storia della filosofia* 9 (1954): 456-484.
[Gaunilon. Language.]

129. ———. "Linguaggio e conoscenza assertiva nel pensiero di Roberto Holkot." *Rivista critica di storia della filosofia* 11 (1956): 15-40.
[Holkot. Language. Truth.]

130. ———. "La teoria del 'Significato totale' della proposizione nel pensiero di Gregorio da Rimini." *Rivista critica di storia della filosofia* 11 (1956): 287-311.
[Gregory of Rimini. Complexe significabilia.]

131. Dambska, Izydora. "Semiotyca wyrazów funkcyjnych w *Dialektyce* Abelarda." *Roczniki Filozoficzne* 16 (1968): 83-91. [P. 91: French

summary under the title "La Sémiotique des 'Dictiones Indefinitae' dans la *Dialectique* d'Abélard."
[Abelard. Syncategoremata.]

132. Decloux, Simon. "La dialectique chez saint Thomas d'Aquin." *Studium Generale* [Berlin] 21 (1968): 258-273.
[Thomas Aquinas.]

133. Deledalle, Gérard. "La logique arabe et ses sources non-aristotéliciennes: remarques sur le petit commentaire d'Al-Fārābī." *Les Études Philosophiques* (1969): 299-318. [No volume number.]
[Arabic logic.]

134. Dinneen, Francis P. [Review of] Jan Pinborg. *Logik und Semantik im Mittelalter. Ein Ueberblick.* In *Historiographia Linguistica* 1 (1974): 221-249.
[Review of 417.]

135. Domański, Juliusz. "Stephani de Reate Tractatus de Secundis Intentionibus e codice Wratislaviensi Bibl. Univ. IV Q IV edidit." *Mediaevalia Philosophica Polonorum* 12 (1966): 67-106.
[Stephanus de Reate. Text. Intentions.]

136. ———. "Jana z Grotkowa. 'De clavibus intentionum'." *Materiały i studia zakładu historii filozofii starożytnej i średniowiecznej* 7 (1967): 3-22. [Journal not seen.]
[John of Grotkow. Text. Intentions.]

137. ———. "Duae quaestiones de intentionibus anonymae e codice Erfordiensi Bibliothecae Amplonianae Q 293." *Mediaevalia Philosophica Polonorum* 14 (1970): 99-112.
[Text. Intentions.]

138. Dominczak, Stanislas. *Les jugements modaux chez Aristote et les scolastiques.* Louvain: Imprimerie "Nova et Vetera," 1923.
[Modal logic.]

139. Ducrot, Oswald. "Quelques implications linguistiques de la théorie médiévale de la supposition." In *History of Linguistic Thought and Contemporary Linguistics*, edited by Herman Parret, pp. 189-227. Berlin, New York: Walter de Gruyter, 1976.
[Supposition.]

140. Duhem, Pierre. "La dialectique d'Oxford et la scolastique italienne." *Bulletin italien* 12 (1912): 6-26, 93-120, 203-223, 289-298. Ibid., 13 (1913): 16-36, 128-146, 297-318.
[Italy. Manuscript sources. Oxford.]

141. Dumitriu, Anton. "Le Problème des Paradoxes au Moyen Age." *Revue Roumaine des Sciences Sociales. Série de Philosophie et Logique* 9 (1965): 113-152.
[Insolubilia.]

142. ———. "Wittgenstein's Solution of the Paradoxes and the Conception of the Scholastic Logician Petrus de Allyaco." *Journal of the History of Philosophy* 12 (1974): 227-237.
[Peter of Ailly. Insolubilia.]

143. ———. "The Logico-Mathematical Antinomies: Contemporary and Scholastic Solutions." *International Philosophical Quarterly* 14 (1974): 309-328.
[Insolubilia.]

144. Duns Scotus, John. *Joannis Duns Scoti Doctoris Subtilis Ordinis Minorum Opera Omnia editio nova juxta editionem Waddingi XII tomos continentem a patribus franciscanis de observantia accurate recognita.* Tomus Primus, Tomus Secundus. Parisiis: L. Vivès, 1891. Reprinted 1969 by Gregg International Publishers Ltd.
[Duns Scotus. Text.]

145. Dürr, Karl. "Aussagenlogik im Mittelalter." *Erkenntnis* 7 (1937-1938): 160-168.
[Abelard. Propositional logic.]
———. See also Part Two: 695.

146. Ebbesen, Sten. "Anonymi Bodleiani in Sophisticos Elenchos Aristotelis Commentarii fragmentum." *Cahiers de l'Institut du moyen-âge grec et latin* 8 (1972): 3-32.
[Text. Aristotle commentary.]

147. ———. "Another Fragment of a Commentary on Aristotle's Sophistici Elenchi. The Anonymous Admont." *Cahiers de l'Institut du moyen-âge grec et latin* 9 (1973): 74-76.
[Text. Aristotle commentary.]

148. ———. "Paris 4720 A. A 12th Century Compendium of Aristotle's Sophistici Elenchi." *Cahiers de l'Institut du moyen-âge grec et latin* 10 (1973): 1-20.
[Text. Aristotle commentary.]

149. ———. "Simon of Faversham on the Sophistici Elenchi." *Cahiers de l'Institut du moyen-âge grec et latin* 10 (1973): 21-28.
[Simon of Faversham. Aristotle commentary.]

150. ——. "Index quaestionum super Sophisticos Elenchos Aristotelis." *Cahiers de l'Institut du moyen-âge grec et latin* 10 (1973): 29-44.
[Aristotle commentary. Manuscript sources.]

151. ——. "Prooemium Mertonense anonymi cuiusdam in Aristotelis Analytica Posteriora commentarii literalis." *Cahiers de l'Institut du moyen-âge grec et latin* 13 (1974): 42-48.
[Text. Aristotle commentary.]

152. ——. "The Summulae, Tractatus VII de fallaciis." In *The Logic of John Buridan*, edited by Jan Pinborg, pp. 139-160. Opuscula Graecolatina (Supplementa Musei Tusculani), vol. 9. Copenhagen: Museum Tusculanum, 1976.
[Buridan. Text. Fallacies.]

153 ——. *Anonymus Aurelianensis II. Aristotle, Alexander, Porphyry and Boethius. Ancient Scholasticism and 12th Century Western Europe. Cahiers de l'Institut du moyen-âge grec et latin* 16. Copenhague, 1976.
[Text. Paralogisms.]

154. Ebbesen, Sten and Jan Pinborg. *Studies in the Logical Writings Attributed to Boethius de Dacia. Cahiers de l'Institut du moyen-âge grec et latin* 3. Copenhague, 1970.
[Boethius of Dacia.]

155. Elie, Hubert. *Le complexe significabile.* Paris: J. Vrin, 1936. [The cover has 1937.]
[Complexe significabilia.]
——. See also Part Two: 701.

156. Enders, Heinz Werner. *Sprachlogische Traktate des Mittelalters und der Semantikbegriff.* Veröffentlichungen des Grabmann-Institutes 20. München, Paderborn, Wien: Ferdinand Schöningh, 1975.
[Language. Meaning. Speculative grammar.]

157. Engels, J. "Het signum naturale in de middeleeuwse filosofische terminologie." *Dialoog* 11 (1970-1971): 131-142. [Not seen.]
[Language.]

158. Faral, Edmond. "Jean Buridan. Notes sur les manuscrits, les éditions et le contenu de ses ouvrages." *Archives d'histoire doctrinale et littéraire du moyen âge* 21ᵉ année (1946): 1-53.
[Buridan. Manuscript sources.]

159. ———. "Jean Buridan: Maître ès arts de l'université de Paris." In *Histoire littéraire de la France*, Tome 38, pp. 462-605. Paris: Imprimerie nationale, 1949.
[Buridan. Manuscript sources.]

160. Feldman, Seymour. "Rescher on Arabic Logic." *The Journal of Philosophy* 61 (1964): 724-734.
[Arabic logic.]
[Discussion of 460.]

161. Ferrater Mora, José. "De Boecio a Alberto de Sajonia: un fragmento de historia de la lógica." *Imago Mundi* [Buenos Aires] Año I, número 3 (1954): 3-22.
[Discussion of 76.]

162. Ferreira, J. "As Súmulas Logicais de Pedro Hispano e as seus comentadores." *Colectânea de Estudos* [Braga] 3 (1952): 360-394.
[Not seen.]
[Peter of Spain.]

163. Fredborg, Karin Margareta. *The Commentary of Thierry of Chartres on Cicero's De Inventione*. Cahiers de l'Institut du moyen-âge grec et latin 7. Copenhague, 1971.
[Thierry of Chartres. Cicero commentary. Rhetoric.]

164. ———. *The Dependence of Petrus Helias' Summa super Priscianum on William of Conches' Glose super Priscianum*. Cahiers de l'Institut du moyen-âge grec et latin 11. Copenhague, 1973.
[Petrus Helias. William of Conches. Priscian commentary.]

165. ———. "Petrus Helias on Rhetoric." *Cahiers de l'Institut du moyen-âge grec et latin* 13 (1974): 31-41.
[Petrus Helias. Rhetoric.]

166. ———. "The Commentaries on Cicero's de Inventione and Rhetorica ad Herennium by William of Champeaux." *Cahiers de l'Institut du moyen-âge grec et latin* 17 (1976): 1-39.
[William of Champeaux. Cicero commentary.]

167. ———. "Buridan's quaestiones super Rhetoricam Aristotelis." In *The Logic of John Buridan*, edited by Jan Pinborg, pp. 47-59. *Opuscula Graecolatina* (Supplementa Musei Tusculani), vol. 9. Copenhagen: Museum Tusculanum, 1976.
[Buridan. Rhetoric.]

168. Gál, Gedeon. "Gualteri de Chatton et Guilelmi de Ockham controversia de Natura Conceptus Universalis." *Franciscan Studies* 27 (1967): 191-212.
 [Chatton. Ockham. Text (Chatton). Universals.]

169. Gandillac, Maurice de. "Le rêve logique de Raymond Lulle." *Revue Philosophique de la France et de l'Étranger* Tome 157, 92e année (1967): 187-221.
 [Lull. Combinatorics.]

170. Gansiniec, Ryszard. "Modi Significandi." *Myśl Filozoficzna* 6 (1956): 80-115.
 [Modi significandi.]

171. García Lescún, Eliseo. "La lógica en el misterio trinitario según Gregorio de Rímini." *Augustinianum* 6 (1966): 528-546.
 [Gregory of Rimini. Paralogisms. Theology.]

172. Garfagnini, Gian Carlo. "'Ratio disserendi' e 'ratiocinandi via': il 'Metalogicon' di Giovanni di Salisbury." *Studi Medievali Serie Terza.* Anno 12 (1971): 915-954.
 [John of Salisbury.]

173. Garin, Eugenio. "La dialettica dal secolo xii ai principî dell'età moderna." *Rivista di filosofia* 49 (1958): 228-253. Reprinted as "Dialettica e retorica dal xii al xvi secolo" in *L'età nuova*, by Eugenio Garin, pp. 43-79. Napoli: Morano, 1969.
 ['Dialectica' (term). Rhetoric.]

174. ———. "La cultura fiorentina nella seconda metà del '300 e i 'barbari britanni'." *La Rassegna della Letteratura Italiana* 64 (1960): 181-195. Reprinted in *L'età nuova*, by E. Garin, pp. 141-166. Napoli: Morano, 1969.
 [Italy.]
 ———. See also Part Two: 709-710.

175. Garlandus Compotista. *Dialectica. First edition of the manuscripts, with an introduction on the life and works of the author and on the contents of the present work* by L. M. de Rijk. Assen: Van Gorcum & Co., 1959.
 [Garlandus Compotista. Text.]

176. Geach, Peter Thomas. *Reference and Generality. An Examination of Some Medieval and Modern Theories.* Ithaca, N.Y.: Cornell University Press, 1962. Emended Edition, 1968.

[Distribution. Reference. Supposition.]
[Discussion: 532.]

177. ——. "A Medieval Discussion of Intentionality." In *Logic, Methodology and Philosophy of Science. Proceedings of the 1964 International Congress*, edited by Y. Bar-Hillel, pp. 425-433. Amsterdam: North-Holland Publishing Company, 1965. Reprinted in *Logic Matters* by P. T. Geach, pp. 129-138. Oxford: Basil Blackwell, 1972.
[Buridan. Intentionality.]

178. ——. "Distribution and *Suppositio*." *Mind* 84 (1976): 432-435.
[Distribution. Supposition.]

179. Geyer, Bernhard. "Zu den Summulae Logicales des Petrus Hispanus und Lambert von Auxerre." *Philosophisches Jahrbuch* 50 (1937): 511-513.
[Lambert of Auxerre. Peter of Spain.]

180. Giacon, Carlo. "La *suppositio* in Guglielmo di Occam e il valore reale delle scienze." In *Arts libéraux et philosophie au moyen âge*, pp. 939-947. Montréal: Institut d'études médiévales, Paris: J. Vrin, 1969.
[Ockham. Supposition.]

181. Gierymski, T. and M. P. Slattery. "Existential Import and 'Latin Averroism'." *Franciscan Studies* 18 (1958): 127-132.
[Siger of Brabant. Averroism. Existential import.]

182. Gilbert, Neal Ward. "Richard de Bury and the 'Quires of Yesterday's Sophisms'." In *Philosophy and Humanism. Renaissance Essays in Honor of Paul Oskar Kristeller*, edited by Edward P. Mahoney, pp. 229-257. Leiden: E. J. Brill, 1976.
[Paris. Sophisms.]
——. See also Part Two: 717-719.

183. Giuliani, Alessandro. "L'élément 'juridique' dans la logique médiévale." *Logique et Analyse*. Nouvelle série 6 (1963): 540-570.
[Law. Logic, history of.]

184. Godfrey, Robert G. "The Language Theory of Thomas of Erfurt." *Studies in Philology* 57 (1960): 22-29.
[Thomas of Erfurt.]

185. ——. "Late Mediaeval Linguistic Meta-Theory and Chomsky's Syntactic Structures." *Word* 21 (1965): 251-256.
[Thomas of Erfurt.]

186. ———. "A Medieval Controversy concerning the Nature of General Grammar." *General Linguistics* 7 (1967): 79-104.
[Speculative grammar.]

187. Goichon, Amélie-Marie. "Une logique moderne à l'époque médiévale: la logique d'Avicenne." *Archives d'histoire doctrinale et littéraire du moyen âge* 22e et 23e années (1947-1948): 53-68.
[Avicenna. Arabic logic.]

188. González, Atanasio. "The Theory of Assertoric Consequences in Albert of Saxony." *Franciscan Studies* 18 (1958): 290-354. Continued: Ibid., 19 (1959): 13-114.
[Albert of Saxony. Consequences.]

189. Grabmann, Martin. "De Thoma Erfordiensi auctore Grammaticae quae Ioanni Duns Scoto adscribitur Speculativae." *Archivium Franciscanum Historicum* 15 (1922): 273-277.
[Duns Scotus. Thomas of Erfurt.]

190. ———. *Neu aufgefundene Werke des Siger von Brabant und Boetius von Dacien. Sitzungsberichte der Bayerischen Akademie der Wissenschaften, Philosophisch-philologische und historische Klasse.* Jahrgang 1924. 2. Abhandlung. München, 1924.
[Boethius of Dacia. Siger of Brabant.]

191. ———. "Die Entwicklung der mittelalterlichen Sprachlogik (Tractatus de Modis Significandi)." In *Mittelalterliches Geistesleben* Band 1, pp. 104-146. München: Max Hueber Verlag, 1926.
[Modi significandi. Speculative grammar.]

192. ———. "Die logischen Schriften des Nikolaus von Paris und ihre Stellung in der Aristotelischen Bewegung des XIII. Jahrhunderts." In *Mittelalterliches Geistesleben* Band 1, pp. 222-248. München: Max Hueber Verlag, 1926.
[Nicholas of Paris. Aristotelianism: medieval.]

193. ———. *Mittelalterliche lateinische Uebersetzungen von Schriften der Aristoteles-Kommentatoren Johannes Philoponos, Alexander von Aphrodisias und Themistios. Sitzungsberichte der Bayerischen Akademie der Wissenschaften, Philosophisch-historische Abteilung* Jahrgang 1929. Heft 7. München, 1929.
[Aristotle commentary.]

194. ———. *Die Introductiones in logicam des Wilhelm von Shyreswood (†nach 1267). Literarhistorische Einleitung und Textausgabe. Sit-*

zungsberichte der Bayerischen Akademie der Wissenschaften. Philosophisch-historische Abteilung. Jahrgang 1937. Heft 10. München, 1937.

[William of Sherwood. Text.]

[Discussion: 318.]

195. ———. Bearbeitungen und Auslegungen der aristotelischen Logik aus der Zeit von Peter Abaelard bis Petrus Hispanus. Mitteilungen aus Handschriften deutscher Bibliotheken. Abhandlungen der Preussischen Akademie der Wissenschaften. Jahrgang 1937. Philosophisch-historische Klasse Nr. 5. Berlin, 1937.

[Aristotelianism: medieval. Logic, history of.]

196. ———. "Kommentare zur aristotelischen Logik aus dem 12. und 13. Jahrhundert im Ms. lat. fol. 624 der Preussischen Staatsbibliothek in Berlin. Ein Beitrag zur Abaelardforschung." Sitzungsberichte der Preussischen Akademie der Wissenschaften. Jahrgang 1938. Philosophisch-historische Klasse, pp. 185-210. Berlin, 1938.

[Abelard. Aristotle commentary.]

197. ———. Die Sophismatenliteratur des 12. und 13. Jahrhunderts mit Textausgabe eines Sophisma des Boetius von Dacien. Beiträge zur Geschichte der Philosophie und Theologie des Mittelalters. Texte und Untersuchungen. Band 36, Heft 1. Münster i.W., 1940.

[Boethius of Dacia. Text. Sophisms.]

198. ———. Thomas von Erfurt und die Sprachlogik des mittelalterlichen Aristotelismus. Sitzungsberichte der Bayerischen Akademie der Wissenschaften. Philosophisch-historische Abteilung. Jahrgang 1943, Heft 2. München, 1943.

[Thomas of Erfurt. Speculative grammar.]

199. ———. "Ein Tractatus de universalibus und andere logische Inedita aus dem 12. Jahrhundert im Cod. lat. 2486 der Nationalbibliothek in Wien." Mediaeval Studies 9 (1947): 56-70.

[Text. Universals.]

200. ———. "Aristoteles im zwoelften Jahrhundert." Mediaeval Studies 12 (1950): 123-162.

[Aristotelianism: medieval. Aristotle: Latin.]

201. ———. "Die geschichtliche Entwicklung der mittelalterlichen Sprachphilosophie und Sprachlogik. Ein Überblick." In Mélanges Joseph de Ghellinck, S.J. Tome 2. Moyen Age, Epoques moderne et

contemporaine, pp. 421-433. Museum Lessianum, Section historique no. 14. Gembloux: Editions J. Duculot, S.A., 1951.
[Language. Speculative grammar.]
[Same as 204.]

202. ——. "Ungedruckte lateinische Kommentare zur aristotelischen Topik aus dem 13. Jahrhundert." In *Mittelalterliches Geistesleben* Band 3, pp. 142-157. München: Max Hueber Verlag, 1956.
[Aristotle commentary.]

203. ——. "Der Kommentar des seligen Jordanus von Sachsen († 1237) zum Priscianus Minor." In *Mittelalterliches Geistesleben* Band 3, pp. 232-242. München: Max Hueber Verlag, 1956.
[Jordan of Saxony. Priscian commentary.]

204. ——. "Die geschichtliche Entwicklung der mittelalterlichen Sprachphilosophie und Sprachlogik—Ein Überblick." In *Mittelalterliches Geistesleben* Band 3, pp. 243-253. München: Max Hueber Verlag, 1956.
[Language. Speculative grammar.]
[Same as 201.]

205. Gracia, Jorge J. E. "Propositions as Premisses of Syllogisms in Medieval Logic." *Notre Dame Journal of Formal Logic* 16 (1975): 545-547.
[William of Sherwood. Propositions. Syllogistic.]
[Discussion of 542.]

206. Green, Romuald. *An Introduction to the Logical Treatise 'De Obligationibus'; with critical texts of William of Sherwood and Walter Burley.* Unpublished dissertation: Catholic University of Louvain, 1963. 2 vols. [Not seen.]
[Burleigh. William of Sherwood. Texts. Obligations.]

207. Green-Pedersen, Niels Jørgen. "On the Interpretation of Aristotle's Topics in the Thirteenth Century." *Cahiers de l'Institut du moyen-âge grec et latin* 9 (1973): 1-46.
[Aristotle commentary.]

208. ——. "The Summulae of John Buridan, Tractatus VI De locis." In *The Logic of John Buridan*, edited by Jan Pinborg, pp. 121-138. *Opuscula Graecolatina* (Supplementa Musei Tueculani), vol. 9. Copenhagen: Museum Tusculanum, 1976.
[Buridan. Text. Topics.]

209. ——. "William of Champeaux on Boethius' Topics according to Orleans Bibl. Mun. 266." *Cahiers de l'Institut du moyen-âge grec et latin* 13 (1974): 13-30.
   [William of Champeaux. Boethius commentary.]

210. Grignaschi, Mario. "Les traductions latines des ouvrages de la logique arabe et l'abrégé d'Alfarabi." *Archives d'histoire doctrinale et littéraire du moyen âge* Tome 39 (1972): 41-107.
   [Albert the Great. Arabic logic.]

211. Gyekye, Kwame. "The Terms 'Prima Intentio' and 'Secuda Intentio' in Arabic Logic." *Speculum* 46 (1971): 32-38.
   [Arabic logic. Intentions.]

212. Haller, Rudolf. "Untersuchungen zum Bedeutungsproblem in der antiken und mittelalterlichen Philosophie." *Archiv für Begriffsgeschichte* 7 (1962): 57-119.
   [Meaning.]

213. Hamblin, Charles Leonard. *Fallacies.* London: Methuen & Co., Ltd., 1970.
   [Fallacies. Obligations. Sophisms.]

214. ——. "An Improved *Pons Asinorum?*" *Journal of the History of Philosophy* 14 (1976): 131-136.
   [Pons asinorum.]

215. Häring, Nikolaus M. "Petrus Lombardus und die Sprachlogik in der Trinitaetslehre der Porretanerschule." In *Miscellanea Lombardiana pubblicata a chiusura delle celebrazioni centenarie organizzate in Novara per onorare Pietro Lombardo a cura del Pontificio Ateneo Salesiano di Torino. Istituto Geografico de Agostini Novara,* pp. 113-127. Novara, 1957.
   [Peter Lombard. Language. Theology.]

216. ——. "Sprachlogische und philosophische Voraussetzungen zum Verständnis der Christologie Gilberts von Poitiers." *Scholastik* 32 (1957): 373-398.
   [Gilbert of Poitiers. Language. Theology.]

217. Heidegger, Martin. *Die Kategorien- und Bedeutungslehre der Duns Scotus.* Tübingen, 1916.
   [Duns Scotus. Thomas of Erfurt.]
   [Translations: 218, 219.]

218. ——. *Traité des catégories et de la signification chez Duns Scot.* Traduit de l'allemand et présenté par Florent Gaboriau. Paris: Gallimard, 1970.
   [Duns Scotus. Thomas of Erfurt.]
   [Translation of 217.]

219. ——. *La dottrina delle categorie e del significato in Duns Scoto.* A cura di Albino Babolin. Roma-Bari: Laterza, 1974. [Not seen.]
   [Duns Scotus. Thomas of Erfurt.]
   [Translation of 217.]

220. Henry, Desmond Paul. "Why 'Grammaticus'?" *Archivum Latinitatis Medii Aevi (Bulletin du Cange)* 28 (1958): 165-180.
   [Anselm. Paronymy.]
   [Review: 301.]

221. ——. "The scope of the logic of St. Anselm." In *L'homme et son destin d'après les penseurs du moyen âge*, pp. 377-383. Louvain: Editions Nauwelaerts, Paris: Béatrice-Nauwelaerts, 1960.
   [Anselm. Modal logic. Paronymy.]

222. ——. "Saint Anselm's *De 'Grammatico'*." *Philosophical Quarterly* 10 (1960): 115-126.
   [Anselm.]

223. ——. "An Anselmian Regress." *Notre Dame Journal of Formal Logic* 3 (1962): 193-198.
   [Anselm.]
   [Review: 301.]

224. ——. "Saint Anselm's Nonsense." *Mind* 72 (1963): 51-61.
   [Anselm.]
   [Review: 301.]

225. ——. "The Early History of *Suppositio.*" *Franciscan Studies* 23 (1963): 205-212.
   [Supposition.]

226. ——. "Ockham, *Suppositio*, and Modern Logic." *Notre Dame Journal of Formal Logic* 5 (1964): 290-292.
   [Ockham. Supposition.]

227. ——. *The De Grammatico of St. Anselm. The Theory of Paronymy.* Notre Dame, Ind.: University of Notre Dame Press, 1964.
   [Anselm. Text. Translation. Paronymy.]
   [Review: 301.]

228. ———. *The Logic of St. Anselm.* Oxford: The Clarendon Press, 1967.
[Anselm.]
[Review: 358.]

229. ———. [Review of] N. Kretzmann (translator): *William of Sherwood's Treatise on Syncategorematic Words.* In *The Philosophical Review* 79 (1970): 568-571.
[Review of 625.]

230. ———. [Reviews of] E. A. Moody, "The Medieval Contribution to Logic"; E. A. Moody, "A Quodlibetal Question of Robert Holkot O.P. on the Problem of the Objects of Knowledge and Belief"; E. A. Moody, "Buridan and a Dilemma of Nominalism." In *The Journal of Symbolic Logic* 35 (1970): 122-124.
[Reviews of 354, 355, 356.]

231. ———. "Saint Anselm as a Logician." In *Sola ratione. Anselm-Studien für Pater Dr.h.c. Franciscus Salesius Schmitt OSB zum 75. Geburtstag am 20 Dezember 1969*, pp. 13-17. Stuttgart-Bad Cannstatt: Friedrich Frommann Verlag (Günther Holzboog), 1970.
[Anselm.]

232. ———. *Medieval Logic and Metaphysics.* London: Hutchinson University Library, 1972.
[Logic, history of.]

233. ———. *Commentary on De Grammatico. The Historical-Logical Dimensions of a Dialogue of St. Anselm's.* Synthèse Historical Library 8. Dordrecht, Holland and Boston, U.S.A.: D. Reidel Publishing Company, 1974.
[Anselm. Text. Translation.]

234. ———. "The Singular Syllogisms of Garlandus Compotista." *Revue internationale de philosophie. Grabmann.* 29e année 113 (1975): 243-270.
[Garlandus Compotista. Syllogistic.]

235. ———. "Negative Terms and Buridan's Syllogistic." In *The Logic of John Buridan*, edited by Jan Pinborg, pp. 115-120. Opuscula Graecolatina (Supplementa Musei Tusculani), vol. 9. Copenhagen: Museum Tusculanum, 1976.
[Buridan. Negative terms. Syllogistic.]

236. Hickman, Larry. *Logical Second Intentions: Late Scholastic*

Theories of Higher Level Predicates. Unpublished dissertation: University of Texas, 1971. [Not seen.]
[Intentions.]
———. See also Part Two: 725-726.

237. Hoffmann, Fritz. "Robert Holcot—Die Logik in der Theologie." In *Miscellanea Mediaevalia.* 2. *Die Metaphysik im Mittelalter,* edited by P. Wilpert, pp. 624-639. Berlin: Walter de Gruyter & Co., 1963.
[Holkot. Theology.]

238. ———. "Modus Significandi. Das Verhältnis von Sprache und Sache in der theologischen Aussage." *Sapienter Ordinare. Festgabe für Erich Kleineidam Erfurter Theologische Studien* 24 (Leipzig, 1969): 147-156.
[Modi significandi. Theology.]

239. ———. "Der Satz als Zeichen der theologischen Aussage bei Holcot, Crathorn und Gregor von Rimini." In *Miscellanea Mediaevalia* 8. *Der Begriff der Repraesentatio im Mittelalter,* edited by A. Zimmermann, pp. 296-313. Berlin, New York: Walter de Gruyter & Co., 1971.
[Crathorn. Holkot. Gregory of Rimini. Theology.]

240. Hubien, Hubert. "John Buridan on the Fourth Figure of the Syllogism." *Revue internationale de philosophie. Grabmann.* 29e année, 113 (1975): 271-285.
[Buridan. Syllogistic.]

241. ———. *Iohannis Buridani Tractatus de Consequentiis. Edition critique.* Philosophes médiévaux, tome XVI. Louvain: Publications Universitaires, Paris: Vander-Oyez, S.A., 1976.
[Buridan. Text. Consequences.]

242. Hunt, Richard William. "Studies on Priscian in the Eleventh and Twelfth Centuries. I. Petrus Helias and His Predecessors." *Mediaeval and Renaissance Studies,* edited by R. Hunt and R. Klibansky, 1 (1941-1943): 194-231.
[Petrus Helias. Priscian commentary.]

243. ———. "Studies on Priscian in the Twelfth Century. II. The School of Ralph of Beauvais." *Mediaeval and Renaissance Studies,* edited by R. Hunt and R. Klibansky, 2 (1950): 1-56.
[Priscian commentary.]

244. ———. "Oxford Grammar Masters in the Middle Ages." *Oxford*

Studies Presented to Daniel Callus. Oxford Historical Society. New Series 16 (Oxford, 1964): 163-193.

[Grammar. Oxford.]

245. ——. "*Absoluta.* The *Summa* of Petrus Hispanus on Priscianus Minor." *Historiographia Linguistica* 2 (1975): 1-23.

[Petrus Hispanus (Grammarian). Priscian commentary.]

246. Inciarte, Fernando. "Die Suppositionstheorie und die Anfänge der extensionalem Semantik." In *Miscellanea Mediaevalia* 9. *Antiqui und Moderni. Traditionsbewusstsein und Fortschrittsbewusstsein im späten Mittelalter,* edited by A. Zimmermann, pp. 126-141. Berlin, New York: Walter de Gruyter, 1974.

[Supposition.]

247. Iriarte, Raúl and Otero, Néstor. "Guillermo de Shyreswood y algunas antecedentes medievales de la filosofía del lenguaje." *Cuadernos del Sur* [Bahía Blanca] 10 (1968-1969): 124-131.

[William of Sherwood. Language.]

248. Isaac, Jean. "La notion de dialectique chez Saint Thomas." *Revue des sciences philosophiques et théologiques* 34 (1950): 481-506.

[Thomas Aquinas.]

249. ——. *Le Peri Hermeneias en occident de Boèce à Saint Thomas. Histoire littéraire d'un traité d'Aristote.* Paris: J. Vrin, 1953.

[Aristotle commentary.]

250. James, Theodore E. "Peter Alboini of Mantua: Philosopher-Humanist." *Journal of the History of Philosophy* 12 (1974): 161-170.

[Peter of Mantua.]

251. Jeauneau, Édouard. "Deux rédactions des gloses de Guillaume de Conches sur Priscien." *Recherches de Théologie ancienne et médiévale* 27 (1960): 212-247.

[William of Conches. Text. Priscian commentary.]

252. Johannes Dacus. *Johannis Daci Opera. Nunc primum edidit Alfredus Otto.* 2 parts. *Corpus philosophorum danicorum medii aevi.* I. Hauniae: G. E. C. Gad, 1955.

[Johannes Dacus. Text.]

253. John of Salisbury. *The Metalogicon of John of Salisbury. A Twelfth-Century Defense of the Verbal and Logical Arts of the Trivium.*

Translated by Daniel D. McGarry. Berkeley and Los Angeles: University of California Press, 1962.
[John of Salisbury. Translation.]

254. Joja, Athanase. "Duns Scot—un Gînditor Progresist în Evul Mediu." In *Studii de logică*, by A. Joja, I, pp. 285-297. Editura Academiei Republicii Populare Romîne, 1960.
[Duns Scotus.]

255. Jolivet, Jean. *Arts du langage et théologie chez Abélard.* Études de philosophie médiévale 57. Paris: J. Vrin, 1969.
[Abelard. Language. Theology.]

256. ——. "Grammaire et langage selon Boèce de Dacie." *Le Moyen Age* 76 (4e série, tome 25) (1970): 307-322.
[Boethius of Dacia. Grammar. Language.]

257. ——. "Comparaison des théories du langage chez Abélard et chez les nominalistes du xive siècle." In *Peter Abelard. Proceedings of the International Conference Louvain May 10-12 1971*, edited by E. M. Buytaert, pp. 163-178. Leuven: University Press, The Hague: Martinus Nijhoff, 1974.
[Abelard. Language. Nominalism.]

258. ——. "Vues médiévales sur les paronymes." *Revue internationale de philosophie. Grabmann.* 29e année, 113 (1975): 222-242.
[Paronymy.]

259. Kelly, L. G. "*De modis generandi*: Points of Contact between Noam Chomsky and Thomas of Erfurt." *Folia Linguistica* 5 (1971): 225-252.
[Thomas of Erfurt. Speculative grammar.]

260. ——. [Reviews of] G. L. Bursill-Hall. *Speculative Grammars of the Middle Ages* and Thomas of Erfurt. *Grammatica Speculativa.* In *Historiographia Linguistica* 1 (1974): 203-219.
[Reviews of 108, 575.]

261. [Kilwardby, Robert.] *The Commentary on 'Priscianus Maior' Ascribed to Robert Kilwardby.* Introduction to the text [by] Jan Pinborg. The problem of the authorship [by] Osmund Lewry. Selected texts edited by K. M. Fredborg, N. J. Green-Pedersen, Lauge Nielsen and Jan Pinborg. *Cahiers de l'Institut du moyen-âge grec et latin* 15. Copenhague, 1975.
[Kilwardby. Text. Priscian commentary.]

262. Kluge, Eike-Henner W. "William of Ockham's Commentary on Porphyry. Introduction and English Translation." *Franciscan Studies* 33 (1973): 171-254. Continued: Ibid., 34 (1974): 306-382.
[Ockham. Translation. Porphyry commentary.]

263. Kneale, Martha. [Review of] L. M. de Rijk. *Logica Modernorum* vol. 1. In *Archiv für Geschichte der Philosophie* 46 (1964): 125-127.
[Review of 469.]

264. Kneale, William. "Modality *De Dicto* and *De Re.*" In *Logic, Methodology and Philosophy of Science. Proceedings of the 1960 International Congress*, edited by E. Nagel, P. Suppes, A. Tarski, pp. 622-635. Stanford, California: Stanford University Press, 1962.
[Modal logic.]

265. ———. [Review of] N. Kretzmann (translator). *William of Sherwood's Introduction to Logic.* In *The Philosophical Review* 77 (1968): 99-101.
[Review of 624.]

266. ———. [Review of] John Buridan. *Sophisms on Meaning and Truth.* In *Mind* 77 (1968): 441-443.
[Review of 104.]

267. Kneale, William and Martha. *The Development of Logic.* Oxford: The Clarendon Press, 1962.
[Logic, history of.]
[Discussion: 53.]

268. Kneepkens, C. H. "'Mulier Quae Damnavit, Salvavit.' A Note on the Early Development of the Relatio simplex." *Vivarium* 14 (1976): 1-25.
[Grammar. Relative terms.]

269. Knudsen, Christian. "Ein Ockhamkritischer Text zu Signifikation und Supposition und zum Verhältnis von erster und zweiter Intention." *Cahiers de l'Institut du moyen-âge grec et latin* 14 (1975): 1-26.
[Chatton. Intentions. Signification. Supposition.]

270. Korcik, Antoni. "Robert Kilwardby jako prekursor Ramusa i Leibniza." *Wydział Nauk Społecznych Polskiej Akademii. Nauk. Sprawozdania z prac naukowych wydziału nauk społecznych.* Rok 5, Zeszyt 4 (26) (1962) [printed 1963]: 47-50.

[Kilwardby. Ramus. Syllogistic.]
———. See also Part Two: 747.

271. Kotarbiński, Tadeusz. *Leçons sur l'histoire de la logique*. Introduction de René Poirier. Traduit du polonais par Anna Posner. Warszawa: Éditions scientifiques de Pologne, Paris: Presses universitaires de France, 1964.
[Lull. Ramus. Nominalism. Universals.]

272. Kretzmann, Norman. "Semantics, History of." In *The Encyclopedia of Philosophy*, edited by P. Edwards, vol. 7, pp. 358-406. New York, London: Macmillan & Free Press, 1967.
[Language. Meaning.]

273. ———. [Review of] L. M. de Rijk. *Logica Modernorum. A Contribution to the History of Early Terminist Logic*. In *The Philosophical Review* 79 (1970): 262-268.
[Review of 469, 470, 471.]

274. ———. "Medieval Logicians on the Meaning of the *Propositio*." *The Journal of Philosophy* 67 (1970): 767-787.
[Propositions. Significate of the proposition.]

275. ———. "Incipit/Desinit." In *Motion and Time, Space and Matter. Interrelations in the History of Philosophy and Science*, edited by Peter K. Machamer and Robert G. Turnbull, pp. 101-136. Columbus: Ohio State University Press, 1976.
[Exponibilia.]

276. Kretzmann, Norman, J. Longeway, E. Stump, J. Van Dyk. [Review of] Peter of Spain. *Tractatus*. First Critical Edition with an Introduction by L. M. de Rijk. In *The Philosophical Review* 84 (1975): 560-567.
[Review of 403.]

277. Kuksewicz, Zdzislaw. "Les Œuvres de Matthieu de Eugubio dans le Ms. 737 de la Bibliothèque Jagellone." *Mediaevalia Philosophical Polonorum* 10 (1961): 40-45.
[Matthew of Eugubio.]

278. ———. "Les œuvres manuscrites d'un Averroïste de Bologne, Jacobus de Placentia." *Rivista di filosofia neo-scolastica* 55 (1963): 211-216.
[Jacob of Placentia.]

279. Lachance, Louis. "Saint Thomas dans l'histoire de la logique." In

Études d'histoire littéraire et doctrinale du XIIIe siècle, première série, pp. 61-103. Paris: J. Vrin, Ottawa: Institut d'études médiévales, 1932.
[Thomas Aquinas.]

280. Lamacchia, Ada. "I *modi significandi* di Martino di Dacia." In *Arts libéraux et philosophie au moyen âge*, pp. 913-921. Montréal: Institut d'études médiévales, Paris: J. Vrin, 1969.
[Martin of Dacia. Modi significandi.]

281. Lambert of Auxerre. Lamberto d'Auxerre. *Logica (Summa Lamberti)*. Prima edizione a cura di Franco Alessio. Firenze: La Nuova Italia Editrice, 1971.
[Lambert of Auxerre. Text.]

282. Leclercq, Jean. "Le 'De Grammatica' de Hugues de Saint-Victor." *Archives d'histoire doctrinale et littéraire du moyen âge* 18e année (1943): 263-322.
[Hugh of St. Victor. Text. Grammar.]

283. ———. "Notes Abélardiennes." *Bulletin de philosophie médiévale* 13 (1971): 68-71.
[Abelard.]

284. Leff, Gordon. *William of Ockham. The metamorphosis of scholastic discourse*. Manchester: Manchester University Press, Totowa, N.J.: Rowman and Littlefield, 1975.
[Ockham.]

285. Lehmann, Paul. *Mitteilungen aus Handschriften VIII. Zu den sprachlogischen Traktaten des Mittelalters. Sitzungsberichte der Bayerischen Akademie der Wissenschaften. Philosophisch-historische Abteilung*. Jahrgang 1944, Heft 2. München, 1944.
[Speculative grammar.]

286. Leuninger, Helen. "Scholastische und transformationelle Sprachtheorie: Die Universalienhypothese." In *History of Linguistic Thought and Contemporary Linguistics*, edited by Herman Parret, pp. 228-237. Berlin, New York: Walter de Gruyter, 1976.
[Modi significandi.]

287. Lohr, Charles H. "*Logica Algazelis*: Introduction and Critical Text." *Traditio* 21 (1965): 223-290.
[Algazel. Text. Arabic logic.]

288. ———. "Medieval Latin Aristotle Commentaries: Authors A-F."

Traditio 23 (1967): 313-413. Continued: '...: Authors G-I." Ibid., 24 (1968): 149-245. "...: Authors: Jacobus-Johannes Juff." Ibid., 26 (1970): 135-216. "...: Authors: Johannes de Kanthi-Myngodus." Ibid., 27 (1971): 251-351. "... Authors: Narcissus-Richardus." Ibid., 28 (1972): 281-396. "... Authors: Robertus-Wilgelmus." Ibid., 29 (1973): 93-197.
[Aristotle commentary. Manuscript sources.]
[Discussion: 627.]

289. ——. *Raimundus Lullus' Compendium logicae Algazelis: Quellen, Lehre und Stellung in der Geschichte der Logik.* Inaugural-Dissertation zur Erlangung der Doktorwürde der Philosophischen Fakultät der Albert-Ludwigs-Universität zu Freiburg im Breisgau. Freiburg im Breisgau, 1967.
[Algazel. Lull. Text (Lull).]

290. ——. "Medieval Latin Aristotle Commentaries. Addenda et Corrigenda." *Bulletin de philosophie médiévale* 14 (1972): 116-126.
[Aristotle commentary. Manuscript sources.]

291. ——. "Ramon Llull. 'Logica brevis'." *Estudios Lulianos* 16 (1972): 1-11.
[Lull.]
[Same as 292.]

292. ——. "Ramón Llull, *Logica brevis.*" *Franciscan Studies* 32 (1972): 144-153.
[Lull.]
[Same as 291.]

293. ——. "Problems of Authorship Concerning Some Medieval Aristotle Commentaries." *Bulletin de philosophie médiévale* 15 (1973): 131-136.
[Aristotle commentary.]

294. ——. "A Note on Manuscripts of Paulus Venetus, Logica." *Bulletin de philosophie médiévale* 15 (1973): 145-146.
[Paul of Venice. Manuscript sources.]

295. ——. "Medieval Latin Aristotle Commentaries, Supplementary Authors." *Traditio* 30 (1974): 119-144.
[Aristotle commentary. Manuscript sources.]

296. ——. "Aristotelica Hispalensia." *Theologie und Philosophie* 50 (1975): 547-564.
   [Aristotle commentary. Manuscript sources.]

297. ——. See also Part Two: 750.

298. Longpré, Ephrem. "La Summula dialectica de Roger Bacon." *Archivum Franciscanum Historicum* 31 (1938): 204-205.
   [Bacon, Roger.]

299. Łukasiewicz, Jan. "Zur Geschichte der Aussagenlogik." *Erkenntnis* 5 (1935): 111-131.
   [Propositional logic.]
   [Translation: 300.]

300. ——. "On the History of the Logic of Propositions." In *Polish Logic 1920-1939*, edited by Storrs McCall, pp. 66-87. Oxford: The Clarendon Press, 1967.
   [Propositional logic.]
   [Translation of 299.]

301. Luschei, Eugene C. [Reviews of] D. P. Henry. *The De Grammatico of St. Anselm. The Theory of Paronymy.* D. P. Henry. "Why 'Grammaticus'?" D. P. Henry. "St. Anselm's Nonsense." D. P. Henry. "The Anselmian Regress." In *The Journal of Symbolic Logic* 36 (1971): 509-513.
   [Reviews of 220, 223, 224, 227.]

302. Maccagnolo, Enzo. "La 'Proprietas Veritatis' in Anselmo d'Aosta." In *Atti del Convegno di Storia della Logica (Parma 8-10 Ottobre 1972)*, pp. 189-193. Padova: Liviana Editrice, 1974.
   [Anselm. Truth.]

303. McCanles, Michael. "Peter of Spain and William of Ockham: From Metaphysics to Grammar." *The Modern Schoolman* 43 (1965-1966): 133-141.
   [Ockham. Peter of Spain.]

304. McDermott, A. Charlene Senape. "Notes on the Assertoric and Modal Propositional Logic of the Pseudo-Scotus." *Journal of the History of Philosophy* 10 (1972): 273-306.
   [Pseudo-Scotus. Consequences. Modal logic.]

305. McInerny, Ralph M. *The Logic of Analogy. An Interpretation of St. Thomas.* The Hague: Martinus Nijhoff, 1961.
   [Thomas Aquinas. Analogy.]

306. ——. "Metaphor and Analogy." *Sciences ecclésiastiques* 16 (1964): 273-289.
[Analogy.]

307. McKeon, Richard. "Rhetoric in the Middle Ages." *Speculum* 17 (1942): 1-32.
[Rhetoric.]

308. Maier, Anneliese. "Ein neues Ockham-Manuskript. (Die Originalform der Expositio aurea?)." *Gregorianum* 28 (1947): 101-133.
[Ockham.]
[Discussion: 72.]

309. Maierù, Alfonso. "Il 'Tractatus de sensu composito et diviso' di Guglielmo Heytesbury." *Rivista critica di storia della filosofia* 21 (1966): 243-263.
[Heytesbury. Composition and division.]

310. ——. "Il problema della verità nelle opere di Guglielmo Heytesbury." *Studi medievali* serie terza, anno 7 (1966): 40-74.
[Heytesbury. Insolubilia. Truth.]

311. ——. "Lo 'Speculum puerorum sive Terminus est in quem' di Riccardo Billingham." *A Giuseppe Ermini. Studi Medievali* serie terza, 10.3 (1969) [printed 1970]: 297-397.
[Billingham. Text.]

312. ——. *Terminologia logica della tarda scolastica*. Roma: Edizioni dell'Ateneo, 1972.
[Logic, history of.]

313. ——. "Il problema del significato nella logica di Pietro da Mantova." In *Miscellanea Mediaevalia 9. Antiqui und Moderni. Traditionsbewusstsein und Fortschrittsbewusstsein im später Mittelalter*, edited by A. Zimmermann, pp. 155-170. Berlin, New York: Walter de Gruyter, 1974.
[Peter of Mantua. Significate of the proposition.]

314. ——. "Significatio et connotatio chez Buridan." In *The Logic of John Buridan*, edited by Jan Pinborg, pp. 101-114. *Opuscula Graecolatina* (Supplementa Musei Tusculani), vol. 9. Copenhagen: Museum Tusculanum, 1976.
[Buridan. Connotation. Signification.]

315. Malatesta, Michele. "La logica delle relazioni nella *Summa Theo-*

logiae di Tommaso d'Aquino." *Rassegna di scienze filosofiche* 26 (1973): 65-83. [Journal not seen.]
[Thomas Aquinas. Relations.]

316. ———. "Logica e ontologia delle relazioni nel pensiero di Tommaso d'Aquino." *Rassegna di scienze filosofiche* 26 (1973): 273-303. [Journal not seen.]
[Thomas Aquinas. Relations.]

317. ———. "La problematica tomistica delle relazioni alla luce della logica matematica e dei moderni indirizzi di pensiero." *Rassegna di scienze filosofiche* 27 (1974): 227-257. [Journal not seen.]
[Thomas Aquinas. Relations.]

318. Malcolm, John. "On Grabmann's Text of William of Sherwood." *Vivarium* 9 (1971): 108-118.
[William of Sherwood.]
[Discussion of 194.]

319. Mandonnet, Félix Pierre. *Siger de Brabant et l'Averroïsme latin au XIIIe siècle*. IIe partie. *Textes inédits*. Deuxième édition revue et augmentée. Les philosophes Belges 7. Louvain: Institut supérieur de philosophie de l'Université, 1908.
[Siger of Brabant. Text.]

320. Manthey, Franz. *Die Sprachphilosophie des hl. Thomas von Aquin und ihre Anwendung auf Probleme der Theologie*. Paderborn, 1937.
[Thomas Aquinas. Language. Theology.]

321. Markowski, Mieczysław. "Le *Commentum in Duos Libros Analyticorum Posteriorum* de Jean Buridan." *Archives d'histoire doctrinale et littéraire du moyen âge* tome 32 (1965): 251-255.
[Buridan. Aristotle commentary.]

322. ———. "Jean Buridan est-il l'auteur des questions sur les 'Seconds Analytiques'?" *Mediaevalia Philosophica Polonorum* 12 (1966): 16-32.
[Buridan. Aristotle commentary.]

323. ———. "Les Questions de Jean Buridan sur les Topiques d'Aristote." *Mediaevalia Philosophica Polonorum* 13 (1968): 3-7.
[Buridan. Aristotle commentary.]

324. ———. *Burydanizm w Polsce w Okresie Przedkopernikańskim.* Studia Copernicana 2. Wrocław-Warszawa-Kraków-Gdańsk; Zakład

Narodowy imiena Ossolińskich Wydawnictwo Polskiej Akademii Nauk, 1971.
[Manuscript sources. Nominalism. Poland.]

325. ——. "Logik und Semantik im 15. Jahrhundert an der Universität Kraków." *Mediaevalia Philosophica Polonorum* 21 (1975): 73-80.
[Cracow. Logic, history of. Meaning.]

326. ——. "Der Gegenstand der Logik gemäss der Krakauer logischen Schriften des 15. Jahrhunderts." *Mediaevalia Philosophica Polonorum* 21 (1975): 81-84.
[Cracow. Manuscript sources.]

327. ——. *Logika. Dzieje filozofii średniówiecznej w Polsce I*. Wrocław-Warszawa-Kraków-Gdańsk: Polska Akademii Nauk, 1975. [Not seen.]
[Logic, history of. Poland.]

328. ——. "Johannes Buridans Kommentare zu Aristoteles' Organon in Mitteleuropas Bibliotheken." In *The Logic of John Buridan*, edited by Jan Pinborg, pp. 9-20. *Opuscula Graecolatina* (Supplementa Musei Tusculani), vol. 9. Copenhagen: Museum Tusculanum, 1976.
[Buridan. Aristotle commentary. Manuscript sources.]

329. Markowski, Mieczysław and Sofia Włodek. *Repertorium commentariorum medii aevi in Aristotelem Latinorum quae in Bibliotheca Iagellonica Cracoviae asservantur.* Wrocław-Warszawa-Kraków-Gdańsk: Zakład Narodowy imiena Ossolińskich Wydawnictwo Polskiej Akademii Nauk, 1974.
[Aristotle commentary. Manuscript sources.]

330. Martin, C. "Walter Burley." In *Oxford Studies Presented to Daniel Callus*, pp. 194-230. Oxford Historical Society. New Series, 16. Oxford, 1964.
[Burleigh.]

331. Martin of Dacia. Martini de Dacia. "De modis significandi (Venezia, Marc. ms. lat. Cl. xiii, n. 54) (Prima edizione a cura di Franco Alessio)." *Rivista critica di storia della filosofia* 11 (1956): 174-205, 312-339.
[Martin of Dacia. Text. Modi significandi.]

332. ——. *Martini de Dacia opera.* Nunc primum edidit H. Roos. Corpus philosophorum danicorum medii aevi 2. Hauniae: G. E. C. Gad, 1961.
[Martin of Dacia. Text.]

333. Mates, Benson. "Pseudo-Scotus on the Soundness of *Consequentiae.*" In *Contributions to Logic and Methodology in Honor of J. M. Bocheński,* edited by A. T. Tymieniecka in collaboration with C. Parsons, pp. 132-141. Amsterdam: North-Holland Publishing Company, 1965.
[Pseudo-Scotus. Consequences.]

334. Matthews, Gareth B. "Ockham's Supposition Theory and Modern Logic." *The Philosophical Review* 73 (1964): 91-99.
[Ockham. Supposition.]

335. ——. "*Suppositio* and Quantification in Ockham." *Nous* 7 (1973): 13-24.
[Ockham. Supposition.]

336. Michałowski, Witold. "Stanowisko Abelarda wzgledem arystotelesowskiej koncepcji prawdy logicznej." *Ruch Filozoficzny* 23 (1964): 60-63. [Not seen.]
[Abelard.]

337. ——. "Pojęcie inferencji i implikacji u Piotra Abelarda." *Ruch Filozoficzny* 25 (1966): 86-88. [Not seen.]
[Abelard. Consequences.]

338. ——. "Zdania ze spójnikami 'si' i 'cum' w logice Boecjusza i Abelarda. (XII Konferencja Grupy Tematycznej Historii Logiki PAN, 22 IV 1966)." *Ruch Filozoficzny* 26 (1968): 216-219. [Journal not seen.]
[Abelard. Propositional logic.]

339. Michaud-Quantin, Pierre. "L'emploi des termes *logica* et *dialectica* au moyen âge." In *Arts libéraux et philosophie au moyen âge,* pp. 855-862. Montréal: Institut d'études médiévales, Paris: J. Vrin, 1969.
['Dialectica' (term). 'Logica' (term).]

340. Mignucci, Mario. "Le Pseudo-Scotiste 'Quaestiones super libros priorum analyticorum Aristotelis' e la sillogistica dello stagirita." In *Studia Scholasticoscotistica* IV. *Acta Congressus Scotistici Internationalis 1966,* pp. 57-71. Roma, 1968.
[Pseudo-Scotus. Aristotle commentary. Syllogistic.]

341. ——. "Albert the Great's Approach to Aristotelian Modal Syllogistic." In *Arts libéraux et philosophie au moyen âge,* pp. 901-911. Montréal: Institut d'études médiévales, Paris: J. Vrin, 1969.
[Albert the Great. Modal logic.]

342. Minio-Paluello, Lorenzo. "The Genuine Text of Boethius' Translation of Aristotle's Categories." *Mediaeval and Renaissance Studies*, edited by R. Hunt and R. Klibansky, 1 (1941-1943): 151-177.
[Aristotle: Latin.]

343. ——. "Note sull'Aristotele latino medievale. IV. La tradizione semitico-latina del testo dei 'secondi analitici'." *Rivista di filosofia neo-scolastica* 43 (1951): 97-124.
[Aristotle: Latin.]

344. ——. "Note sull'Aristotele latino medievale. V. L'ignota versione Moerbekana dei 'secondi analitici' usata da S. Tomaso. VI. Boezio, Giacomo Veneto, Guglielmo di Moerbeke, Jacques Lefèvre d'Etaples e gli 'Elenchi Sofistici'." *Rivista di filosofia neo-scolastica* 44 (1952): 389-411.
[Le Fèvre d'Étaples. William of Moerbeke. Aristotle: Latin.]

345. ——. "The 'Ars disserendi' of Adam of Balsham 'Parvipontanus'." *Mediaeval and Renaissance Studies*, edited by R. Hunt and R. Klibansky, 3 (1954): 116-169.
[Adam of Balsham.]

346. ——. *Twelfth Century Logic Texts and Studies. I. Adam Balsamiensis Parvipontani Ars Disserendi (Dialectica Alexandri)*. Roma: Edizioni di Storia e Letteratura, 1956.
[Adam of Balsham. Text.]

347. ——. *Twelfth Century Logic Texts and Studies. II. Abaelardiana Inedita. 1. Super Periermenias XII-XIV. 2. Sententie secundum M. Petrum.* Roma: Edizioni di Storia e Letteratura, 1958.
[Abelard. Texts. Aristotle commentary.]

348. Miralles, M. García. "Escritos filosóficos de San Vicente Ferrer." *Estudios Filosóficos* [Santander] 4 (1955): 279-284.
[Vincent Ferrer.]

349. Mohan, Gaudens E. "Incipits of Logical Writings of the xiiith-xvth Centuries." *Franciscan Studies* 12 (1952): 349-489.
[Manuscript sources.]

350. ——. *Incipits of Philosophical Writings in Latin of the xiiith-xvth Centuries.* Unpublished manuscript: St. Bonaventure University, New York.
[Manuscript sources.]

351. Mondin, B. "La logica di S. Tommaso d'Aquino." *Rivista di filosofia neo-scolastica* anno 60 (1968): 261-271.
[Thomas Aquinas.]

352. Moody, Ernest Addison. *The Logic of William of Ockham.* London: Sheed & Ward, 1935. Reissued: New York: Russell & Russell, 1965.
[Ockham.]

353. ———. *Truth and Consequence in Mediaeval Logic.* Amsterdam: North-Holland Publishing Company, 1953.
[Consequences. Truth.]

354. ———. "A Quodlibetal Question of Robert Holkot, O.P., on the Problem of the Objects of Knowledge and of Belief." *Speculum* 39 (1964): 53-74.
[Holkot.]
[Review: 230.]
[Reprinted: 359.]

355. ———. "Buridan and a Dilemma of Nominalism." In *Harry Austryn Wolfson Jubilee Volume on the Occasion of His Seventy-Fifth Birthday. English Section.* Volume 2, pp. 577-596. Jerusalem: American Academy for Jewish Research, 1965.
[Buridan. Intentionality. Sophisms.]
[Review: 230.]
[Reprinted: 359.]

356. ———. "The Medieval Contribution to Logic." *Studium Generale* 19 (1966): 443-452.
[Logic, history of.]
[Review: 230.]
[Reprinted: 359.]

357. ———. "Medieval Logic" under "Logic, History of." In *The Encyclopedia of Philosophy*, edited by P. Edwards, vol. 4, pp. 528-534. New York-London: Macmillan & Free Press, 1967.
[Logic, history of.]

358. ———. [Review of] D. P. Henry. *The Logic of St. Anselm.* In *The Philosophical Review* 79 (1970): 274-279.
[Review of 228.]

359. ———. *Studies in Medieval Philosophy, Science and Logic. Collected Papers 1933-1969.* Berkeley, Los Angeles, London: University of California Press, 1975.
[Reprints of 354, 355, 356.]

360. Morduhai-Boltovskoi, D. "Insolubiles in scholastica et paradoxos de infinito de nostro tempore." *Wiadomości Matematyczne* 47 (1939): 111-117.
 [Insolubilia.]

361. Moreno, Alberto J. "Lógica medieval." *Sapientia* [Buenos Aires] 16 (1961): 246-263.
 [Logic, history of.]

362. Morscher, Edgar. "Der Begriff 'consequentia' in der mittelalterlichen Logik." *Archiv für Begriffsgeschichte* 15 (1971): 133-139.
 [Consequences.]

363. Muckle, J. T. "Utrum theologia sit scientia. A Quodlibet Question of Robert Holcot O.P. edited by J. T. Muckle C.S.B." *Mediaeval Studies* 20 (1958): 127-153.
 [Holkot. Text. Theology.]

364. Mullally, Joseph P. *The Summulae Logicales of Peter of Spain.* Notre Dame, Ind.: The University of Notre Dame Press, 1945. Reprinted, 1960.
 [Peter of Spain. Text. Translation.]

365. Mullick, M. "Does Ockham accept Material Implication?" *Notre Dame Journal of Formal Logic* 12 (1971): 117-124.
 [Ockham. Implication.]

366. Muñoz Delgado, Vicente. "La lógica antigua y medieval a la luz de la logística." *Salmanticensis* 4 (1957): 503-541.
 [Logic, history of.]

367. ——. "La lógica de las proposiciones en el Pseudo-Escoto." *Estudios* 23 (1967): 163-181.
 [Pseudo-Scotus. Propositional logic.]

368. ——. "El 'Breviloquium Logicae' de Nicolás Eymerich (1320-1399)." *Estudios filosóficos* 22 (1973): 3-28.
 [Eymerich.]

369. ——. "Introducción al patrimonio escolástico de lógica." *Cuadernos Salmantinos de filosofía* 2 (1975): 45-75.
 [Logic, history of.]
 ——. See also Part Two: 762-798.

370. Murphy, James Jerome. *Rhetoric in the Middle Ages. A History of Rhetorical Theory from Saint Augustine to the Renaissance.*

Berkeley, Los Angeles, London: University of California Press, 1974.
[Rhetoric.]

371. Narbutt, Olgierd. "De quelques problèmes de la logique médiévale." *Notre Dame Journal of Formal Logic* 17 (1976): 361-374.
[Consequences. Syllogistic.]

372. Nehring, Alfonso. "A Note on Functional Linguistics in the Middle Ages." *Traditio* 9 (1953): 430-434.
[Martin of Dacia.]

373. Nicolau d'Olwer, L. "Sur la date de la *Dialectica* d'Abélard." *Revue du moyen âge latin* 1 (1945): 375-390.
[Abelard.]

374. Nielsen, Lauge. "On the Doctrine of Logic and Language of Gilbert Porreta and his Followers." *Cahiers de l'Institut du moyen-âge grec et latin* 17 (1976): 40-69.
[Gilbert of Poitiers. Language.]

375. Nuchelmans, Gabriel. *Theories of the Proposition. Ancient and Medieval Conceptions of the Bearers of Truth and Falsity.* Amsterdam-London: North-Holland Publishing Company, 1973.
[Complexe significabilia. Propositions. Significate of the proposition. Truth.]

376. Ockham, William. *The Tractatus de Praedestinatione et de Praescientia Dei et de Futuris Contingentibus of William Ockham. Edited with a Study on the Mediaeval Problem of a Three-Valued Logic by Philotheus Boehner.* St. Bonaventure, N.Y.: The Franciscan Institute, 1945.
[Ockham. Text. Future contingents.]

377. ———. *Summa Logicae Pars Prima.* Edited by Philotheus Boehner. St. Bonaventure, N.Y., Louvain: The Franciscan Institute, 1951. Reprinted (Paderborn, Germany) 1957.
[Ockham. Text.]

378. ———. *Summa Logicae Pars Secunda et Tertiae Prima.* Edited by Philotheus Boehner. St. Bonaventure, N.Y., Louvain, Paderborn: The Franciscan Institute, 1954.
[Ockham. Text.]

379. ———. *Expositionis in Libros Artis Logicae prooemium et Expositio in*

Librum Porphyrii de Praedicabilibus. Edited by E. A. Moody. St. Bonaventure, N.Y.: The Franciscan Institute, 1965.
[Ockham. Text. Porphyry commentary.]

380. ——. *Predestination, God's Foreknowledge and Future Contingents.* Translated with an introduction, notes and appendices by M. McCord Adams and N. Kretzmann. New York: Appleton Century Crofts, 1969.
[Ockham. Translation. Future contingents.]

381. ——. [Wilhelm]. *Suma Logiczna* wyboru dokonał, z oryginału łacińskiego prazełożył, wstępem i przypisami opatrzył Tadeusz Włodarczyk. Redaktor naukowy Irena Tarnowska. Państwowe Wydawnictwo Naukowe: Warszawa, 1971.
[Ockham. Translation.]

382. ——. *Ockham's Theory of Terms: Part I of the Summa Logicae.* Translated and Introduced by M. J. Loux. Notre Dame, Ind.: University of Notre Dame Press, 1974.
[Ockham. Translation. Terms.]
[Review: 396.]

383. ——. *Venerabilis Inceptoris Guillelmi de Ockham Summa Logicae ediderunt Philotheus Boehner, Gedeon Gál, Stephanus Brown. Opera Philosophica 1* of: *Guillelmi de Ockham Opera Philosophica et Theologica.* St. Bonaventure, N.Y.: Editiones Instituti Franciscani Universitatis S. Bonvaventurae, 1974.
[Ockham. Text.]
[Review: 395.]

384. O'Donnell, J. Reginald. "The Syncategoremata of William of Sherwood." *Mediaeval Studies* 3 (1941): 46-93.
[William of Sherwood. Text. Syncategoremata.]

385. ——. "Themistius' Paraphrasis of the Posterior Analytics in Gerard of Cremona's translation." *Mediaeval Studies* 20 (1958): 239-315.
[Themistius (Latin). Text.]

386. ——. "The Commentary of Giles of Rome on the Rhetoric of Aristotle." In *Essays in Medieval History presented to Bertie Wilkinson*, edited by T. A. Sandquist and M. R. Powicke, pp. 139-156. Toronto: University of Toronto Press, 1969.
[Giles of Rome. Aristotle commentary. Rhetoric.]

387. O'Mahony, B. E. "A Mediaeval Semantic. The Scholastic 'Tractatus

de Modis Significandi'." *Laurentianum* 5 (1964): 448-486. [Journal not seen.]
[Modi significandi.]

388. ———. "The Medieval Treatise on Modes of Meaning." *Philosophical Studies* [Ireland] 14 (1965): 117-138.
[Modi significandi.]

389. Ottaviano, Carmelo. *Le 'Quaestiones super libro Praedicamentorum' di Simone di Faversham. Dal* MS. *Ambrosiano 'C.161.Inf.' Memorie della Reale Accademia Nazionale dei Lincei. Classe di scienze morali, storiche e filologiche* (Anno CCCXXVII) Serie VI. Volume III. Fascicolo IV. Roma, 1930.
[Simon of Faversham. Text. Aristotle commentary.]

390. Otto, Alfred. "Magister Johannes Dacus und seine Schriften." *Classica et Mediaevalia* 13 (1952): 73-86.
[Johannes Dacus.]

391. Pagallo, Giulio F. "Nota sulla *Logica* di Paolo Veneto: la critica alla dottrina del 'complexe significabile' di Gregorio da Rimini." In *Atti del* XII *congresso internazionale di filosofia*, vol. 9, pp. 183-191. Firenze, 1960.
[Gregory of Rimini. Paul of Venice. Complexe significabilia.]

392. Palacz, Ryszard. "Gualterii Burleii Quaestio: Utrum contradictio sit maxima oppositio (ms. Vat. Ottob. 318 f 141va-145vb)." *Mediaevalia Philosophica Polonorum* 11 (1963): 128-139.
[Burleigh. Text. Opposition.]

393. ———. "Bespośrednia recepcja arystotelizmu w *Metalogiconie* Jana z Salisbury." *Studia mediewistyzcne* 5 (1964): 191-251.
[John of Salisbury.]

394. ———. "La 'Positio de Universalibus' d'Étienne de Palecz." *Mediaevalia Philosophica Polonorum* 14 (1970): 113-129.
[Stephen of Palecz. Text. Universals.]

395. Panaccio, Claude. [Review of] G. de Ockham. *Summa Logicae.* Ed. par Ph. Boehner, G. Gal et S. Brown. *Dialogue* 15 (1976): 525-527.
[Review of 383.]

396. ———. [Review of] *Ockham's Theory of Terms. Part 1 of the Summa Logicae.* Translated and introduced by Michael J. Loux. In *Dialogue* 15 (1976): 527-530.
[Review of 382.]

397. Paqué, Ruprecht. *Das Pariser Nominalistenstatut. Zur Entstehung des Realitätsbegriffs der Neuzeitlichen Naturwissenschaft. (Occam, Buridan und Petrus Hispanus, Nikolaus von Autrecourt und Gregor von Rimini)*. Berlin: Walter de Gruyter & Co., 1970.
[Complexe significabilia. Supposition. Terms.]

398. Paul of Venice. *Logica Magna (Tractatus de Suppositionibus)*. Edited and translated by A. R. Perreiah. St. Bonaventure, N.Y.: The Franciscan Institute, 1971.
[Paul of Venice. Text. Translation. Supposition.]

399. Perreiah, Alan R. "Approaches to Supposition-Theory." *The New Scholasticism* 45 (1971): 381-408.
[Supposition.]

400. ———. "Buridan and the Definite Description." *Journal of the History of Philosophy* 10 (1972): 153-160.
[Buridan. Definite description. Reference.]]

401. Peter of Spain. *Petri Hispani Summulae Logicales quas e codice manu scripto Reg. Lat. 1205 edidit I. M. Bocheński*. Torino: Marietti, 1947.
[Peter of Spain. Text.]
[Discussion: 437.]

402. ———. *Tractatus Syncategorematum and Selected Anonymous Treatises*. Translated by J. P. Mullally. With an Introduction by J. P. Mullally and R. Houde. Milwaukee, Wisc.: The Marquette University Press, 1964.
[Peter of Spain. Translation. Consequences. Exponibilia. Insolubilia. Syncategoremata.]

403. ———. *Tractatus called afterwards Summule Logicales*. First critical edition from the manuscripts with an introduction by L. M. de Rijk. Assen: Van Gorcum, 1972.
[Peter of Spain. Text.]
[Reviews: 38, 276.]

404. Pinborg, Jan. "Interjektionen und Naturlaute. Petrus Heliae und ein Problem der antiken und mittelalterlichen Sprachphilosophie." *Classica et Mediaevalia* 22 (1961) [published 1962]: 117-138.
[Petrus Helias. Language.]

405. ———. "Eine neue sprachlogische Schrift des Simon de Dacia." *Scholastik* 39 (1964): 220-232.
[Simon of Dacia.]

406. ——. "Mittelalterliche Sprachtheorien. Was heisst Modus Significandi?" In *Fides Quaerens Intellectum. Festskrift tilegnet Heinrich Roos S.J.*, Særnummer af *Catholica*, pp. 66-84. København: Arne Frost-Hansens Forlag, 1964.
[Modi significandi.]

407. ——. "Three Unedited Sophismata of Siger of Kortrijk." *Classica et Mediaevalia* 26 (1965): 276-278.
[Siger of Courtrai. Text. Sophisms.]

408. ——. *Die Entwicklung der Sprachtheorie im Mittelalter. Beiträge zur Geschichte der Philosophie und Theologie des Mittelalters. Texte und Untersuchungen*. Band 42, Heft 2. Münster: Aschendorff, Kopenhagen: Arne Frost-Hansen, 1967.
[Language. Speculative grammar.]

409. ——. "Walter Burleigh on the Meaning of Propositions." *Classica et Mediaevalia* 28 (1967): 394-404. [Date also given as 1968. Vol. printed in 1970.]
[Burleigh. Significate of the proposition.]

410. ——. [Review of] L. M. de Rijk. *Logica Modernorum. Vol. 2.* In *Vivarium* 6 (1968): 155-158.
[Review of 470, 471.]

411. ——. "Die Erfurter Tradition im Sprachdenken des Mittelalters." In *Miscellanea Mediaevalia 5. Universalismus und Partikularismus im Mittelalter*, edited by P. Wilpert, pp. 173-185. Berlin: Walter de Gruyter & Co., 1968.
[Germany. Language.]

412. ——. "Topik und Syllogistik im Mittelalter." In *Sapienter Ordinare. Festgabe für Erich Kleineidam. Erfurter Theologische Studien* 24 (Leipzig 1969): 157-178.
[Syllogistic. Topics.]

413. ——. "Pour une interprétation moderne de la théorie linguistique du moyen âge." *Acta Linguistica Hafniensia* 12 (1969): 238-243.
[Language.]

414. ——. "Miszellen zur mittelalterlichen lateinischen Grammatik." *Cahiers de l'Institut du moyen-âge grec et latin* 1 (1969): 13-20.
[Grammar.]

415. ——. "Bezeichnung in der Logik des XIII. Jahrhunderts." In

Miscellanea Mediaevalia 8. *Der Begriff der Repraesentatio im Mittelalter*, edited by A. Zimmermann, pp. 238-281. Berlin, New York: Walter de Gruyter & Co., 1971.
[Meaning. Reference.]

416. ———. "The Sophismata of Radulphus Brito." *Cahiers de l'Institut du moyen-âge grec et latin* 8 (1972): 33-34.
[Radulphus Brito. Sophisms.]

417. ———. *Logik und Semantik im Mittelalter. Ein Ueberblick.* Stuttgart-Bad Cannstatt: Friedrich Frommann Verlag Günther Holzboog KG, 1972.
[Language. Logic, history of.]
[Reviews: 17, 134.]

418. ———. "Petrus de Alvernia on Porphyry." *Cahiers de l'Institut du moyen-âge grec et latin* 9 (1973): 47-67.
[Peter of Alvernia. Porphyry commentary.]

419. ———. "Radulphus Brito on the Elenchi." *Cahiers de l'Institut du moyen-âge grec et latin* 9 (1973): 80-82.
[Radulphus Brito. Aristotle commentary.]

420. ———. "Some Syntactical Concepts in Medieval Grammar." In *Classica et Mediaevalia. Francisco Blatt Septuagenario Dedicata. Classica et Mediaevalia Dissertationes* 9, pp. 496-509. Copenhagen: Gyldendal, 1973.
[Grammar.]

421. ———. "Textsemantische Probleme in der Sprachtheorie und Logik des Mittelalters." In *Sprache und Sprachverständnis in religiöser Rede. Zum Verhältnis von Theologie und Linguistic*, herausgegeben von Thomas Michels und Ansgar Paus, pp. 135-148, diskussion pp. 148-169. Internationales Forschungszentrum für Grundfragen der Wissenschaften Salzburg. Zwölftes Forschungsgespräch. Salzburg, München: Universitätsverlag Anton Pustet, 1973.
[Language. Logic, history of. Theology.]

422. ———. "The Ms. Bruxelles, B. Royale 3540-47, Radulphus Brito and the Sophistici Elenchi." *Cahiers de l'Institut du moyen-âge grec et latin* 10 (1973): 45-47.
[Radulphus Brito. Aristotle commentary.]

423. ———. "A New Ms. of the Questions on the Posteriora Analytica

Attributed to Petrus de Alvernia (Clm 8005) with the Transcription of Some Questions Related to Problems of Meaning." *Cahiers de l'Institut du moyen-âge grec et latin* 10 (1973): 48-62.
[Peter of Alvernia. Text. Aristotle commentary. Meaning.]

424. ———. [Review of] Thomas of Erfurt. *Grammatica Speculativa.* Translation and Commentary by G. L. Bursill-Hall. In *Lingua* 34 (1974): 369-373.
[Review of 575.]

425. ———. "Zum Begriff der Intentio Secunda, Radulphus Brito, Hervaeus Natalis und Petrus Aureoli in Diskussion." *Cahiers de l'Institut du moyen-âge grec et latin* 13 (1974): 49-59.
[Hervaeus Natalis. Peter Aureol. Radulphus Brito. Intentions.]

426. ———. "Petrus de Alvernia on the Categories." *Cahiers de l'Institut du moyen-âge grec et latin* 14 (1974): 40-46.
[Peter of Alvernia. Aristotle commentary.]

427. ———. "A Note on Some Theoretical Concepts of Logic and Grammar." *Revue internationale de philosophie. Grabmann.* 29e année, 113 (1975): 286-296.
[Grammar. Language.]

428. ———. "Die Logik der Modistae." *Studia Mediewistyczne* 16 (1975): 39-97.
[Speculative grammar.]

429. ———. "Radulphus Brito's Sophism on Second Intentions." *Vivarium* 13 (1975): 119-152.
[Radulphus Brito. Text. Intentions.]

430. ———. "The Summulae, Tractatus I De introductionibus." In *The Logic of John Buridan*, edited by Jan Pinborg, pp. 71-90. *Opuscula Graecolatina* (Supplementa Musei Tusculani), vol. 9. Copenhagen: Museum Tusculanum, 1976.
[Buridan. Text. Signification.]

431. ———. "Some Problems of Semantic Representations in Medieval Logic." In *History of Linguistic Thought and Contemporary Linguistics*, edited by Herman Parret, pp. 254-278. Berlin, New York: Walter de Gruyter, 1976.
[Ockham. Meaning.]

432. Pires, Celestino. "Logica et methodus apud Petrum Hispanum." In *Arts libéraux et philosophie au moyen âge*, pp. 895-900. Montréal:

Institut d'études médiévales, Paris: J. Vrin, 1969.
[Peter of Spain.]

433. Platzeck, Erhard-Wolfram. "Die Lullsche Kombinatorik." *Franziskanische Studien* 34. Jahr (1952): 32-60, 377-407.
[Lull. Combinatorics.]

434. ———. "La combinatoria luliana." *Revista de filosofia* 12 (1953): 575-609. Continued: Ibid., 13 (1954): 125-165.
[Lull. Combinatorics.]

435. ———. "Raimund Lulls auffassung von der Logik." *Estudios Lulianos* 2 (1958): 5-36, 273-296.
[Lull. Logic, concept of.]

436. Poveda, E. "El tratado *De Suppositionibus dialecticis* de San Vicente Ferrer y su significación historica en la cuestión de los universales." *Anales del Seminario de Valencia* 3 (1963): 5-88. [Moncada, Spain: Metropolitana de Valencia.] [Not seen.]
[Vincent Ferrer. Supposition. Universals.]

437. Pozzi, Lorenzo. "Nota sull'edizione Bocheński delle *Summulae* di Pietro Ispano." *Rivista critica di storia della filosofia* 23 (1968): 330-342.
[Peter of Spain.]
[Discussion of 401.]

438. ———. *Studi di logica antica e medievale.* Padova, 1974. [Not seen.]
[Logic, history of.]

439. Prantl, Carl. *Michael Psellus und Petrus Hispanus. Eine Rechtfertigung.* Leipzig, 1867.
[Peter of Spain.]

440. ———. *Geschichte der Logik im Abendlande.* 4 volumes. Leipzig, 1855-1867. Photographic reproduction by Akademische Druk- u. Verlagsanstalt Graz, Austria, 1955.
[Logic, history of.]
[Translation: 441.]

441. ———. *Storia della logica in occidente. Età medievale. Parte prima. Dal secolo VII al secolo XII.* Versione italiana, condotta sopra la seconda edizione tedesca da Ludovico Limentani. Firenze: "La Nuova Italia" Editrice, 1937.
[Logic, history of.]
[Translation of 440.]

442. Prentice, Robert. "Univocity and Analogy according to Scotus's *Super Libros Elenchorum Aristotelis.*" *Archives d'histoire doctrinale et littéraire du moyen âge* tome 35, 43ᵉ année (1968): 39-64.
 [Duns Scotus. Analogy. Aristotle commentary.]

443. Preti, Giulio. "Dialettica terministica e probabilismo nel pensiero medievale." In *La crisi dell'uso dogmatico della ragione.* Saggi di A. Banfi, M. Dal Pra, G. Preti, P. Rossi, a cura di Antonio Banfi, pp. 61-97. Roma, Milano: Fratelli Bocca Editori, 1953.
 [Logic, history of.]

444. ——. "Studi sulla logica formale nel medioevo. I. Lo svolgimento della logica terministica medievale." *Rivista critica di storia della filosofia* 8 (1953): 346-373.
 [Logic, history of.]

445. ——. "Studi sulla logica formale nel medioevo. II. Natura (oggetto, scopi, methodo) della logica." *Rivista critica di storia della filosofia* 8 (1953): 680-697.
 [Logic, concept of.]

446. ——. "La dottrina della *vox significativa* nella semantica terministica classica." *Rivista critica di storia della filosofia* 10 (1955): 223-264.
 [Meaning.]

447. Price, Robert. "William of Ockham and *Suppositio Personalis.*" *Franciscan Studies* 30 (1970): 131-140.
 [Ockham. Supposition.]

448. Prior, Arthur Norman. "The *Parva Logicalia* in Modern Dress." *Dominican Studies* 5 (1952): 78-87.
 [Peter of Spain.]

449. ——. "Modality de dicto and modality de re." *Theoria* 18 (1952): 174-180.
 [Modal logic.]

450. ——. "On Some *Consequentiae* in Walter Burleigh." *The New Scholasticism* 27 (1953): 433-446.
 [Burleigh. Consequences.]

451. ——. "Some Problems of Self-Reference in John Buridan." *Proceedings of the British Academy* 48 (1962): 281-296. Reprinted in *Studies in Philosophy. British Academy Lectures*, selected and in-

troduced by J. N. Findlay, pp. 241-259. London: Oxford University Press, 1966.
[Buridan. Insolubilia.]

452. ———. [Review of] John Buridan. *Sophisms on Meaning and Truth.* In *The Philosophical Review* 77 (1968): 516-519.
[Review of 104.]

453. ———. "The Possibly-true and the Possible." *Mind* 78 (1969): 481-492.
[Buridan. Truth.]

454. Qadir, C. A. "An Early Islamic Critic of Aristotelian Logic: Ibn Taimiyyah." *International Philosophical Quarterly* 8 (1968): 498-512.
[Arabic logic.]

455. Rached, Amina. "Un exemple de logique simplifiée en Catalogne au XIIIe siècle: raisonnement imagé et anecdote chez Raymond Lulle." *Revue philosophique de la France et de l'Étranger* tome 157, 92e année (1967): 256-263.
[Lull.]

456. Reina, Maria Elena. "Il problema del linguaggio in Buridano. I. Voci e concetti." *Rivista critica di storia della filosofia* 14 (1959): 367-417.
[Buridan. Meaning.]

457. ———. *Il problema del linguaggio in Buridano.* Vicenza: Tipografia Editoriale Vittore Gualandi, 1959.
[Buridan. Language.]

458. ———. "Il problema del linguaggio in Buridano. II. Significazione e verità." *Rivista critica di storia della filosofia* 15 (1960): 141-165.
[Buridan. Signification. Truth.]

459. ———. "Il problema del linguaggio in Buridano. III. Il linguaggio." *Rivista critica di storia della filosofia* 15 (1960): 238-264.
[Buridan. Language.]

460. Rescher, Nicholas. *Studies in the History of Arabic Logic.* Pittsburgh: University of Pittsburgh Press, 1963.
[Arabic logic.]
[Discussion: 160.]

461. ———. "Avicenna on the Logic of 'Conditional' Propositions." *Notre Dame Journal of Formal Logic* 4 (1963): 48-58.
[Avicenna. Arabic logic.]

462. ———. *The Development of Arabic Logic.* Pittsburgh: University of Pittsburgh Press, 1964.
    [Arabic logic.]

463. ———. *Galen and the Syllogism. An Examination of the Thesis that Galen Originated the Fourth Figure of the Syllogism in the Light of New Data from Arabic Sources Including an Arabic Text Edition and Annotated Translation of Ibn al-Ṣalāḥ's Treatise "On the Fourth Figure of the Categorical Syllogism."* Pittsburgh: University of Pittsburgh Press, 1966.
    [Arabic logic. Syllogistic.]

464. ———. *Temporal Modalities in Arabic Logic.* Dordrecht, Holland: D. Reidel Publishing Company, 1967.
    [Arabic logic. Time.]

465. Richard of Campsall. *The Works of Richard of Campsall.* Volume 1. *Questiones super Librum Priorum Analeticorum* MS *Gonville and Caius 668**. Edited by Edward A. Synan. Toronto: Pontifical Institute of Mediaeval Studies, 1968.
    [Richard of Campsall. Text. Aristotle commentary.]
    [Includes reprint of 562.]

466. Richards, T. J. "The Two Doctrines of Distribution." *Australasian Journal of Philosophy* 49 (1971): 290-302.
    [Distribution. Supposition.]

467. Rijk, Lambertus Marie de. "Some new evidence on twelfth century logic: Alberic and the School of Mont Ste Geneviève (Montani)." *Vivarium* 4 (1966): 1-57.
    [Logic, history of.]

468. ———. "Some notes on the mediaeval tract *De insolubilibus*, with the edition of a tract dating from the end of the twelfth century." *Vivarium* 4 (1966): 83-115.
    [Text. Insolubilia.]

469. ———. *Logica Modernorum. A Contribution to the History of Early Terminist Logic.* Vol. 1. *On the Twelfth Century Theories of Fallacy.* Assen: Van Gorcum, 1962.
    [Texts. Fallacies.]
    [Review: 263, 273.]

470. ———. *Logica Modernorum. A Contribution to the History of Early*

Terminist Logic. Vol. 2. Part One. *The Origin and Early Development of the Theory of Supposition*. Assen: Van Gorcum, 1967.
[Supposition.]
[Reviews: 273, 410.]

471. ———. *Logica Modernorum. A Contribution to the History of Early Terminist Logic*. Vol. 2, Part Two. *The Origin and Early Development of the Theory of Supposition. Texts and Indices*. Assen: Van Gorcum, 1967.
[Text. Supposition.]
[Reviews: 273, 410.]

472. ———. "On the genuine text of Peter of Spain's *Summule logicales.*" *Vivarium* 6 (1968): 1-34, 69-101. Continued: Ibid., 7 (1969): 8-61, 120-162; Ibid., 8 (1970): 10-55.
[Peter of Spain.]

473. ———. "Significatio y suppositio en Pedro Hispano." *Pensamiento* 25 (1969): 225-234.
[Peter of Spain. Signification. Supposition.]

474. ———. "Die Bedeutungslehre der Logik im 13. Jahrhundert und ihr Gegenstück in der metaphysischen Spekulation." In *Miscellanea Mediaevalia 7. Methoden in Wissenschaft und Kunst des Mittelalters*, edited by A. Zimmermann, pp. 1-22. Berlin: Walter de Gruyter & Co., 1970.
[Logic, history of. Meaning.]

475. ———. "On the Life of Peter of Spain, the Author of the *Tractatus*, called afterwards *Summule logicales.*" *Vivarium* 8 (1970): 123-154.
[Peter of Spain.]

476. ———. "The Development of *suppositio naturalis* in Mediaeval Logic." *Vivarium* 9 (1971): 71-107. Continued: Ibid., 11 (1973): 43-79.
[Supposition.]

477. ———. "Some Thirteenth Century Tracts on the Game of Obligation." *Vivarium* 12 (1974): 94-123. Continued: Ibid., 13 (1975): 22-54; Ibid., 14 (1976): 26-49.
[William of Sherwood. Texts (Anonymous: obligations, William of Sherwood). Obligations. Sophisms.]

478. ———. "The Place of Billingham's 'Speculum puerorum' in 14th and

15th Century Logical Tradition with the Edition of Some Alternative Tracts." *Studia Mediewistyczne* 16 (1975): 99-153.
[Billingham. Text.]

479. ———. "La Signification de la Proposition (Dictum Propositionis) chez Abélard." *Studia Mediewistyczne* 16 (1975): 155-161.
[Abelard. Significate of the proposition.]

480. ———. "Logica Cantabrigiensis—A Fifteenth Century Cambridge Manual of Logic." *Revue internationale de philosophie. Grabmann.* 29e année, 113 (1975): 297-315.
[Cambridge. Manuscript sources.]

481. ———. "Another 'Speculum puerorum' attributed to Richard Billingham. Introduction and Text." *Medioevo* 1 (1975): 203-235.
[Billingham. Text.]

482. ———. "Richard Billingham's Works on Logic." *Vivarium* 14 (1976): 121-138.
[Billingham. Manuscript sources.]

483. ———. "On Buridan's Doctrine of Connotation." In *The Logic of John Buridan*, edited by Jan Pinborg, pp. 91-100. *Opuscula Graecolatina* (Supplementa Musei Tusculani), vol. 9. Copenhagen: Museum Tusculanum, 1976.
[Buridan. Connotation.]

484. Ritter, Gerhard. *Studien zur Spätscholastik. I. Marsilius von Inghen und die okkamistische Schule in Deutschland. Sitzungsberichte der Heidelberger Akademie der Wissenschaften. Philosophisch-historische Klasse.* Jahrgang 1921, 4. Abhandlung. Heidelberg, 1921.
[Marsilius of Inghen. Germany. Nominalism.]

485. Rivero, Maria Luisa. "Antecedents of Contemporary Logical and Linguistic Analysis in Scholastic Logic." *Foundations of Language* 10 (1973): 55-64.
[Composition and division.]

486. ———. "Modalities and Scope in Scholastic Logic from a Linguistic Point of View." *Acta Linguistica Hafniensia* 15 (1974): 133-152.
[Modal logic.]

487. ———. "Early Scholastic Views on Ambiguity: Composition and Division." *Historiographia Linguistica* 2 (1975): 25-47.
[Composition and division.]

488. ——. "La ambigüedad de los verbos modales: una visión histórica." *Revista española de lingüística.* Año 5, Fasc. 2 (1975): 401-422.
[Modal logic.]

489. ——. "William of Sherwood on Composition and Division." *Historiographia Linguistica* 3 (1976): 17-36.
[William of Sherwood. Composition and division.]

490. Rivière, Jean. "Saint Anselme logicien." *Revue des sciences religieuses* 17 (1937): 306-315.
[Anselm.]

491. Robert, S. "Rhetoric and Dialectic: According to the First Latin Commentary on the Rhetoric of Aristotle." *The New Scholasticism* 31 (1957): 484-498. Reprinted in: *Aristotle: The Classical Heritage of Rhetoric,* edited by Keith V. Erickson, pp. 90-101. Metuchen N.J.: The Scarecrow Press Inc., 1974.
[Giles of Rome. Aristotle commentary. Rhetoric.]

492. [Roberts], Louise Nisbet. "Formalism of Terminist Logic in the Fourteenth Century." *Tulane Studies in Philosophy* 1 (1952): 107-112.
[Buridan. Consequences.]

493. Roberts, Louise Nisbet. "Every Proposition is False. A Medieval Paradox." *Tulane Studies in Philosophy* 2 (1953): 95-102.
[Insolubilia.]

494. ——. "Classification of Suppositions in Medieval Logic." *Tulane Studies in Philosophy* 5 (1956): 79-86.
[Supposition.]

495. ——. "A Chimera is a Chimera: A Medieval Tautology." *Journal of the History of Ideas* 21 (1960): 273-278.
[Buridan. Signification.]

496. ——. "Supposition: A Modern Application." *The Journal of Philosophy* 57 (1960): 173-182.
[Supposition.]

497. ——. "Notes on a Past Logic of Time." *Tulane Studies in Philosophy* 16 (1967): 123-128.
[Time.]

498. Robins, Robert Henry. *Ancient and Mediaeval Grammatical Theory*

in Europe, with Particular Reference to Modern Linguistic Doctrines. London: G. Bell & Sons, Ltd., 1951.
[Grammar. Speculative grammar.]

499. ———. *A Short History of Linguistics.* London: Longmans, 1967.
[Language. Speculative grammar.]

500. Robles, Laureano. "Notas Históricas al 'De Modalibus' de Sto Tomás." *Teorema* 4 (1974): 419-450. [Journal not seen.]
[Thomas Aquinas. Text. Translation. Modal logic.]

501. Roos, Heinrich. "Martinus de Dacia und seine Schrift De Modis Significandi. Ein Beitrag zur Geschichte der Dänischen Sprachlogik im Mittelalter." *Classica et Mediaevalia* 8 (1946): 87-115.
[Martin of Dacia. Modi significandi.]

502. ———. "Sprachdenken im Mittelalter." *Classica et Mediaevalia* 9 (1948) [1947]: 200-215.
[Language.]

503. ———. *Die Modi Significandi des Martinus de Dacia. Forschungen zur Geschichte der Sprachlogik im Mittelalter. Beiträge zur Geschichte der Philosophie und Theologie des Mittelalters.* Band 37, Heft 2. Münster, Westfalen: Aschendorff, Kopenhagen: Arne Frost-Hansen, 1952.
[Martin of Dacia. Modi significandi. Speculative grammar.]

504. ———. "Die Stellung der Grammatik im Lehrbetrieb des 13. Jahrhunderts." In *Artes Liberales, von der antiken Bildung zur Wissenschaft des Mittelalters,* herausgegeben von Josef Koch, pp. 94-106. *Studien und Texte zur Geistesgeschichte des Mittelalters* 5. Leiden, Köln: E. J. Brill, 1959.
[Grammar.]

505. ———. "Das Sophisma des Boetius von Dacien 'Omnis homo de necessitate est animal' in doppelter Redaktion." *Classica et Mediaevalia* 23 (1962): 178-197.
[Boethius of Dacia. Text. Sophisms.]

506. ———. "Ein unbekanntes Sophisma des Boetius de Dacia." *Scholastik* 38 (1963): 378-391.
[Boethius of Dacia. Sophisms.]

507. ———. "Neue Handschriften-Funde zu den Modi significandi des Martinus de Dacia." *Theologie und Philosophie* 41 (1966): 243-246.
[Martin of Dacia. Manuscript sources. Modi significandi.]

508. ———. "Den moderne sprogfilosofi og middelalderen." *Catholica* 25 (1968): 113-122.
 [Language.]

509. ———. "Le *Trivium* à l'université au xiiie siècle." In *Arts libéraux et philosophie au moyen âge*, pp. 193-197. Montréal: Institut d'études médiévales, Paris: J. Vrin, 1969.
 [Logic, history of. Speculative grammar.]

510. ———. "Neuentdeckte Sophismata zum Formproblem." *Theologie und Philosophie* 46 (1971): 248-255.
 [Sophisms.]

511. Rose, Valentin. "Pseudo-Psellus und Petrus Hispanus." *Hermes. Zeitschrift für classische Philologie* 2 (1867): 146-147.
 [Peter of Spain.]

512. Ross, James F. "Analogy as a Rule of Meaning for Religious Language." *International Philosophical Quarterly* 1 (1961): 468-502.
 [Thomas Aquinas. Analogy. Modi significandi.]

513. Rotta, Paolo. *La filosofia del linguaggio nella patristica e nella scolastica.* Torino, 1909.
 [Language.]

514. Roure, M. L. "La problématique des propositions insolubles au xiiie siècle et au début du xive, suivie de l'édition des traités de W. Shyreswood, W. Burleigh et Th. Bradwardine." *Archives d'histoire doctrinale et littéraire du moyen âge* 37 (1970): 205-326.
 [Bradwardine. Burleigh. William of Sherwood. Texts. Insolubilia.]
 ———. See also Part Two: 837.

515. Rubió Balaguer, Jordi. "La Lògica del Gazzali, posada en rims per En Ramón Lull." *Anuari de l'Institut d'Estudis Catalans* 5 (1913-1914): 311-354. [Journal not seen.]
 [Algazel. Lull. Text (Lull).]

516. Rüstow, Alexander. *Der Lügner: Theorie/Geschichte und Auflösung.* Leipzig: B. G. Teubner, 1910.
 [Insolubilia.]

517. Saarnio, Uuno. "Betrachtungen über die scholastische Lehre der Wörter als Zeichen." *Acta Academiae Paedogogicae Jyväskyläensis* 17 (1959): 215-249.
 [Signification. Terms.]

518. Sagal, P. T. "Refuting and Defending Supposition Theory." *The New Scholasticism* 47 (1973): 84-87.
[Ockham. Supposition.]

519. Salamucha, Jan. "Logika zdań u Wilhelma Ockhama." *Przegląd Filozoficzny* 38 (1935): 208-239.
[Ockham.]
[Translation: 521.]

520. ———. "Pojawienie się zagadnień antynomialnych na gruncie logiki średniowiecznej." *Przegląd Filozoficzny* 40 (1937): 68-89, 320-343.
[Insolubilia.]

521. ———. "Die Aussagenlogik bei Wilhelm Ockham. (Aus dem Polnischen übersetzt von Johannes Bendiek O.F.M.)." *Franziskanische Studien* 32 (1950): 97-134.
[Ockham. Propositional logic.]
[Translation of 519.]

522. Salmon, D. "The Mediaeval Latin Translations of Alfarabi's Works." *The New Scholasticism* 13 (1939): 245-261.
[Albert the Great. Alfarabi.]

523. Salus, Peter Henry. "Pre-Pre-Cartesian linguistics." In *Papers from the Fifth Regional Meeting of the Chicago Linguistic Society April 18-19, 1969*, pp. 429-434. Chicago: Department of Linguistics, University of Chicago, 1969.
[Anselm. Peter of Spain. Petrus Helias. Siger of Courtrai.]

524. ———. "Universal Grammar 1000-1850." In *History of Linguistic Thought and Contemporary Linguistics*, edited by Herman Parret, pp. 85-101. Berlin, New York: Walter de Gruyter, 1976.
[Grammar. Speculative grammar.]

525. Saw, Ruth Lydia. "William of Ockham on Terms, Propositions, Meaning." *Proceedings of the Aristotelian Society* 42 (1941-1942): 45-64.
[Ockham. Meaning. Propositions. Terms.]

526. Schepers, Heinrich. "Holkot contra dicta Crathorn. I. Quellenkritik und biographische Auswertung der Bakkalareatsschriften zweier Oxforder Dominikaner des xiv. Jahrhunderts." *Philosophisches Jahrbuch* 77 (1970): 320-354.
[Crathorn. Holkot.]

527. ———. "Holkot contra dicta Crathorn. II. Das 'significatum per

propositionem'. Aufbau und Kritik einer nominalistischen Theorie über den Gegenstand des Wissens." *Philosophisches Jahrbuch* 79 (1972): 106-136.
[Crathorn. Holkot. Significate of the proposition.]

528. ———. "Holkot contra dicta Crathorn. Corrigenda." *Philosophisches Jahrbuch* 79 (1972): 361.
[Crathorn. Holkot.]

529. Schmidt, Robert William. *The Domain of Logic according to Saint Thomas Aquinas.* The Hague: Martinus Nijhoff, 1966.
[Thomas Aquinas. Logic, concept of.]
[Review: 589.]

530. Schüssler, Ursula. "Das Verhältnis der Dialektik Peter Abaelards zur modernen Logik." *Mittellateinisches Jahrbuch* 9 (1973): 39-47.
[Abelard. Propositional logic.]

531. Scott, Theodore Kermit. "John Buridan on the Objects of Demonstrative Science." *Speculum* 40 (1965): 654-673.
[Buridan. Significate of the proposition.]

532. ———. "Geach on Supposition Theory." *Mind* 75 (1966): 586-588.
[Supposition.]
[Discussion of 176.]

533. Seaton, Wallace K. *An Edition and Translation of the Consequentiae [Tractatus de Consequentiis] by Ralph Strode, Fourteenth Century Logician and Friend of Geoffrey Chaucer.* Unpublished dissertation. University of California, Berkeley, 1973.
[Strode. Text. Translation. Consequences.]

534. Seńko, Władysław. "Le commentaire de Thomas Sutton sur les Catégories d'Aristote dans le ms. IV.Q.3 de la bibliothèque de l'université de Wrocław." *Mediaevalia Philosophica Polonorum* 4 (1959): 35-38.
[Sutton. Aristotle commentary.]

535. Shapiro, Herman and Murray J. Kitely. "Walter Burley's *De Relativis.*" *Franciscan Studies* 22 (1962): 155-171.
[Burleigh. Text. Relative terms.]

536. Shehaby, Nabil. *The Propositional Logic of Avicenna. A Translation from al-Shifā': al-Qiyās.* Synthèse Historical Library, 7. Dordrecht, Holland and Boston, U.S.A.: D. Reidel Publishing Company, 1973.
[Avicenna. Translation. Arabic logic. Propositional logic.]

537. Siger of Courtrai. *Zeger van Kortrijk, commentator van Perihermeneias; inleidende studie en tekstuitgave*, with an English summary, door C. Verhaak. Verhandelingen van de Koninklijke Vlaamse Academie voor Wetenschappen, Letteren en Schone Kunsten van België. Klasse der Letteren. Jaargang 26, No. 52. Brussel, 1964.
[Siger of Courtrai. Text. Aristotle commentary.]

538. Simon of Dacia. *Simonis Daci Opera.* Nunc Primum edidit Alfredus Otto. *Corpus Philosophorum Danicorum Medii Aevi* 3. Hauniae: G. E. C. Gad, 1963.
[Simon of Dacia. Text.]

539. Simon of Faversham. *Magistri Simonis Anglici sive de Faversham: Opera Omnia I. Opera Logica Tomus Prior. Quaestiones super libro Porphyrii. Quaestiones super libro Praedicamentorum. Quaestiones super libro Perihermeneias.* Cura et studio Paschalis Mazzarella. Padova: CEDAM, 1957. [Not seen.]
[Simon of Faversham. Text. Aristotle commentary. Porphyry commentary.]

540. Simonin, H. "Les 'Summulae Logicales' de Petrus Hispanus." *Archives d'histoire doctrinale et littéraire du moyen âge* 5e année (1930): 267-278.
[Peter of Spain.]

541. Simplicius. *Commentaire sur les catégories d'Aristote. Traduction de Guillaume de Moerbeke.* Édition critique. Tome I, par A. Pattin. Corpus Latinum Commentariorum in Aristotelem Graecorum V/1. Louvain: Publications universitaires de Louvain, Paris: Éditions Béatrice-Nauwelaerts, 1971.
[William of Moerbeke. Text. Aristotle commentary. Simplicius: Latin.]

542. Sirridge, Mary J. "William of Sherwood on Propositions and their Parts." *Notre Dame Journal of Formal Logic* 15 (1974): 462-464.
[William of Sherwood. Propositions.]
[Discussion: 205.]

543. Spade, Paul Vincent. "An Anonymous Tract on Insolubilia from MS Vat. Lat. 674. An Edition and Analysis of the Text." *Vivarium* 9 (1971): 1-18.
[Text. Insolubilia.]

544. ———. "The Treatises *On Modal Propositions* and *On Hypothetical*

Propositions by Richard Lavenham." *Mediaeval Studies* 35 (1973): 49-59.

[Lavenham. Text. Modal logic. Propositional logic.]

545. ———. "The Origins of the Mediaeval *Insolubilia* Literature." *Franciscan Studies* 33 (1973): 292-309.

[Insolubilia.]

546. ———. "Ockham on Self-Reference." *Notre Dame Journal of Formal Logic* 15 (1974): 298-300.

[Ockham. Insolubilia.]

547. ———. "Five Logical Tracts by Richard Lavenham." In *Essays in Honour of Anton Charles Pegis*, edited by J. R. O'Donnell, pp. 70-124. Toronto: Pontifical Institute of Mediaeval Studies, 1974.

[Lavenham. Text.]

548. ———. "Ockham's Rule of Supposition: Two Conflicts in His Theory." *Vivarium* 12 (1974): 63-67.

[Ockham. Supposition.]

549. ———. "Ockham's Distinctions between Absolute and Connotative Terms." *Vivarium* 13 (1975): 55-76.

[Ockham. Connotation. Terms.]

550. ———. "Notes on Some Manuscripts of Logical and Physical Works by Richard Lavenham." *Manuscripta* 19 (1975): 139-146.

[Lavenham. Manuscript sources.]

551. ———. *The Mediaeval Liar: A Catalogue of the Insolubilia-literature*. Subsidia Mediaevalia 5. Toronto: Pontifical Institute of Mediaeval Studies, 1975.

[Insolubilia. Manuscript sources.]

552. ———. "Some Epistemological Implications of the Burley-Ockham Dispute." *Franciscan Studies* 35 (1975): 212-222.

[Burleigh. Ockham. Supposition.]

553. ———. "William Heytesbury's Position on 'Insolubles': One Possible Source." *Vivarium* 14 (1976): 114-120.

[Heytesbury. Insolubilia.]

554. ———. "Robert Fland's *Consequentiae*: An Edition." *Mediaeval Studies* 38 (1976): 54-84.

[Fland. Text. Consequences.]

———. See also Part Two: 846.

555. Stapper, Richard. *Papst Johannes XXI. Ein Monographie.* 4.4 of *Kirchengeschichtliche Studien* herausgegeben von Dr. Knöpfler, Dr. Schrörs, Dr. Sdralek. Münster i.W.: Verlag von Heinrich Schöningh, 1898.
[Peter of Spain.]

556. Stéfanini, Jean. "Les modistes et leur apport à la théorie de la grammaire et du signe linguistique." *Semiotica* 8 (1973): 263-275.
[Grammar. Modi significandi.]

557. Stiker, Henri-Jacques. "Une théorie linguistique au moyen âge: l'école modiste." *Revue des sciences philosophiques et théologiques* 56 (1972): 585-616.
[Thomas of Erfurt. Speculative grammar.]

558. Streveler, Paul Andrew. *The Problem of Future Contingents from Aristotle through the Fifteenth Century, with Particular Emphasis upon Medieval Views.* Unpublished dissertation: The University of Wisconsin, 1970.
[Future contingents.]

559. Swieżawski, Stefan. "Les intentions premières et les intentions secondes chez Jean Duns Scot." *Archives d'histoire doctrinale et littéraire du moyen âge* 9e année (1934): 205-260.
[Duns Scotus. Intentions.]
———. See also Part Two: 847.

560. Swiniarski, John. "A New Presentation of Ockham's Theory of Supposition with an Evaluation of Some Contemporary Criticisms." *Franciscan Studies* 30 (1970): 181-217.
[Ockham. Supposition.]
[Discussion: 653.]

561. Synan, Edward A. "The Universal and Supposition in a *Logica* attributed to Richard of Campsall." In *Nine Mediaeval Thinkers: A Collection of Hitherto Unedited Texts*, edited by J. R. O'Donnell, pp. 183-232. Toronto: Pontifical Institute of Mediaeval Studies, 1955.
[Richard of Campsall. Text. Supposition. Universals.]

562. ———. "Richard of Campsall's First Question on the 'Prior Analytics'." *Mediaeval Studies* 23 (1961): 305-323.
[Richard of Campsall. Text. Aristotle commentary.]
[Reprinted: 465.]

563. ———. "Sixteen Sayings by Richard of Campsall on Contingency and Foreknowledge." *Mediaeval Studies* 24 (1962): 250-262.
[Richard of Campsall. Text. Future contingents.]

564. ———. "The 'insolubilia' of Roger Nottingham O.F.M." *Mediaeval Studies* 26 (1964): 257-270.
[Roger of Nottingham. Text. Insolubilia.]

565. ———. "Master Peter Bradlay on the 'Categories'." *Mediaeval Studies* 29 (1967): 273-327.
[Bradlay. Text. Aristotle commentary.]

566. ———. "A Question by Peter Bradlay on the 'Prior Analytics'." *Mediaeval Studies* 30 (1968): 1-21.
[Bradlay. Text. Aristotle commentary.]

567. Thomas Aquinas. *S. Thomae Aquinatis. Opuscula Omnia ... cura et studio P. Mandonnet. Tomus Quintus. Opuscula Spuria.* Parisiis: P. Lethielleux, 1927.
[Thomas Aquinas. Text.]

568. ———. *Opuscula Omnia necnon opera minora. Tomus Primus. Opuscula philosophica.* Edited by Joannes Perrier. Paris: P. Lethielleux, 1949.
[Thomas Aquinas. Text.]

569. ———. *Opuscula Philosophica Cura et Studio* P. Fr. Raymundi M. Spiazzi O.P. Torino: Marietti, 1954. Reprinted 1973.
[Thomas Aquinas. Text.]

570. ———. *In Aristotelis Libros Peri Hermeneias et Posteriorum Analyticorum Expositio cum textu ex recensione leonina* cura et studio P. Fr. Raymundi M. Spiazzi O.P. Torino: Marietti, 1955. *Editio Secunda*: Torino: Marietti, 1964.
[Thomas Aquinas. Text. Aristotle commentary.]

571. ———. *Exposition of the Posterior Analytics of Aristotle.* Translated by Pierre Conway. Québec: La Librairie Philosophique M. Doyon, 1956.
[Thomas Aquinas. Translation. Aristotle commentary.]

572. ———. *Quaestiones Disputatae.* Vol. 1. *De Veritate*, edited by R. M. Spiazzi. Torino: Marietti, 1964.
[Thomas Aquinas. Text. Truth.]

573. ———. *Commentary on the Posterior Analytics of Aristotle.* Translated by F. R. Larcher. Albany, New York: Magi Books, Inc., 1970.
[Thomas Aquinas. Translation. Aristotle commentary.]

574. Thomas of Erfurt: see Duns Scotus, John. *Grammaticae speculativae nova editio.* Cura et studio P. Fr. Mariani Fernández García. Ad Claras Aquas: Quaracchi, 1902.
[Thomas of Erfurt. Text. Speculative grammar.]

575. ——. *Grammatica Speculativa of Thomas of Erfurt.* An edition, with translation and commentary by G. L. Bursill-Hall. London: Longman, 1972.
[Thomas of Erfurt. Text. Translation. Speculative grammar.]
[Reviews: 260, 424.]

576. Thomas, Ivo. "St. Vincent Ferrer's *De Suppositionibus.*" *Dominican Studies* 5 (1952): 88-102.
[Vincent Ferrer. Supposition.]

577. ——. "Kilwardby on Conversion." *Dominican Studies* 6 (1953): 56-76.
[Kilwardby. Text. Conversion.]

578. ——. "Maxims in Kilwardby." *Dominican Studies* 7 (1954): 129-146.
[Kilwardby. Consequences.]

579. ——. "A 12th Century Paradox of the Infinite." *The Journal of Symbolic Logic* 23 (1958): 133-134.
[Adam of Balsham. Infinite, paradox of.]

580. ——. [Review of] William of Sherwood. *Introduction to Logic.* In *Philosophy of Science* 34 (1967): 295-296.
[Review of 624.]
——. See also Part Two: 848-853.

581. Thomson, S. Harrison. "Robert Kilwardby's Commentaries *In Priscianum* and *In Barbarismum Donati.*" *The New Scholasticism* 12 (1938): 52-65.
[Kilwardby. Donatus commentary. Priscian commentary.]

582. Thurot, Charles. "De la logique de Pierre d'Espagne." *Revue Archéologique Nouvelle série* 5e année 10 (1864): 267-281.
[Peter of Spain.]

583. ——. *Notices et extraits de divers manuscrits latins pour servir à l'histoire des doctrines grammaticales au moyen âge.* Vol. 22. Pt. 2. *Notices et extraits des manuscrits de la Bibliothèque Impériale et autres bibliothèques....* Paris: Imprimerie Impériale, 1868.
[Texts. Grammar.]

584. Tonelli, Giorgio. "Der historische Ursprung der kantischen Termini 'Analytik' und 'Dialektik'." *Archiv für Begriffsgeschichte* 7 (1962): 120-139.
['Dialectica' (term).]

585. Traina, Mariano. "La dialettica in Giovanni Duns Scoto." In *Arts libéraux et philosophie au moyen âge*, pp. 923-938. Montréal: Institut d'études médiévales, Paris: J. Vrin, 1969.
[Duns Scotus.]

586. Trentman, John A. *Simple Supposition and Ontology: A Study in Fourteenth-Century Logical Theory.* Unpublished dissertation: University of Minnesota, 1964.
[Supposition.]

587. ——. "Vincent Ferrer on the Logician as *Artifex Intellectualis.*" *Franciscan Studies* 25 (1965): 322-337.
[Vincent Ferrer.]

588. ——. "Leśniewski's Ontology and Some Medieval Logicians." *Notre Dame Journal of Formal Logic* 7 (1966): 361-364.
[Predication.]

589. ——. [Review of] R. W. Schmidt. *The Domain of Logic according to Saint Thomas Aquinas.* In *Dialogue* 7 (1968): 318-320.
[Review of 529.]

590. ——. "Predication and Universals in Vincent Ferrer's Logic." *Franciscan Studies* 28 (1968): 47-62.
[Vincent Ferrer. Predication. Universals.]

591. ——. "Extraordinary Language and Medieval Logic." *Dialogue* 7 (1968): 286-291.
[Language.]

592. ——. "Vincent Ferrer and His Fourteenth-Century Predecessors on a Problem of Intentionality." In *Arts libéraux et philosophie au moyen âge*, pp. 949-956. Montréal: Institut d'études médiévales, Paris: J. Vrin, 1969.
[Vincent Ferrer. Intentionality.]

593. ——. "Ockham on Mental." *Mind* 79 (1970): 586-590.
[Ockham. Mental language.]

594. ——. "Speculative Grammar and Transformational Grammar: A Comparison of Philosophical Presuppositions." In *History of*

Linguistic Thought and Contemporary Linguistics, edited by Herman Parret, pp. 279-301. Berlin, New York: Walter de Gruyter, 1976.
[Speculative grammar.]
———. See also Part Two: 854.

595. Turnbull, Robert G. "Ockham's Nominalistic Logic: Some Twentieth Century Reflections." *The New Scholasticism* 36 (1962): 313-329.
[Ockham. Descent to singulars.]

596. Tweedale, Martin. "Abailard and Non-Things." *Journal of the History of Philosophy* 5 (1967): 329-342.
[Abelard. Significate of the proposition. Truth.]

597. ———. [Reviews of] O. Bird. "The Logical Interest of the Topics as seen in Abelard." O. Bird. "The Formalizing of the Topics in Mediaeval Logic." O. Bird. "Topic and Consequence in Ockham's Logic." O. Bird. "The Re-Discovery of the Topics." In *The Journal of Symbolic Logic* 34 (1969): 497-499.
[Reviews of 48, 49, 50, 51.]

598. ———. [Review of] I. Boh. "An Examination of Ockham's Aretetic Logic." In *The Journal of Symbolic Logic* 34 (1969): 499.
[Review of 85.]

599. ———. *Abailard on Universals*. Amsterdam, New York, Oxford: North-Holland Publishing Company, 1976.
[Abelard. Significate of the proposition. Truth. Universals.]
———. See also Part Two: 855.

600. Vasoli, Cesare. *Ricerche preliminari sulla logica occamista*. Firenze: Olschki Editore, 1952. [Not seen.]
[Ockham.]

601. ———. "Pietro Alboini da Mantova 'scolastico' della fine del Trecento e un'epistola di Coluccio Salutati." *Rinascimento* seconda serie 3 (1963): 3-21.
[Peter of Mantua.]

602. ———. "Intorno al Petrarca ed ai logici 'moderni'." In *Miscellanea Mediaevalia 9. Antiqui und Moderni. Traditionsbewusstsein und Fortschrittsbewusstsein im späten Mittelalter*, edited by A. Zimmermann, pp. 142-154. Berlin, New York: Walter de Gruyter, 1974.
[Italy.]
———. See also Part Two: 857-873.

603. Veatch, Henry. "St. Thomas' Doctrine of Subject and Predicate. A Possible Starting Point for Logical Reform and Renewal." In *St. Thomas Aquinas (1274-1974) Commemorative Studies*, foreword by Etienne Gilson. Vol. 2, pp. 401-422. Toronto: Pontifical Institute of Mediaeval Studies, 1974.
[Thomas Aquinas. Predication.]

604. Verbeke, Gérard. *Een onvoltooide commentaar van Thomas van Aquino (Peri Hermeneias). Mededelingen van de koninklijke vlaamse Academie voor wetenschappen, letteren en schone kunsten van België. Klasse der Letteren*. Jaargang 22, 1960, Nr 8. Brussel.
[Thomas Aquinas. Text. Aristotle commentary.]

605. Verhaak, C. "Het Perihermeneias-commentaar van Zeger van Kortrijk: Vragen over authenticiteit en literaire afhankelijkheid." *Bijdragen: Tijdschrift voor filosofie en theologie* 22 (1961): 161-185.
[Siger of Courtrai.]

606. Versace, Giovanni. "La Teoria della 'Suppositio Simplex' in Occam e in Burley." In *Atti del Convegno di Storia della Logica (Parma 8-10 Ottobre 1972)*, pp. 195-202. Padova: Liviana Editrice, 1974.
[Burleigh. Ockham. Supposition.]

607. Vescovini, Graziella Federici. "A propos de la diffusion des œuvres de Jean Buridan en Italie du xive au xvie siècle." In *The Logic of John Buridan*, edited by Jan Pinborg, pp. 21-45. *Opuscula Graecolatina* (Supplementa Musei Tusculani), vol. 9. Copenhagen: Museum Tusculanum, 1976.
[Buridan. Italy. Manuscript sources.]

608. Vincent Ferrer. *De Supposicionibus Dialectices* in *Œuvres de Saint Vincent Ferrier*, 1, edited by Le Père Fages. Paris, 1909.
[Vincent Ferrer. Text. Supposition.]

609. Wallerand, G. *Les Œuvres de Siger de Courtrai. Étude critique et textes inédits*. Les Philosophes Belges. Textes et Études 8. Louvain, 1913.
[Siger of Courtrai. Text.]

610. Washell, Richard F. "Logic, Language and Albert the Great." *Journal of the History of Ideas* 34 (1973): 445-450.
[Albert the Great. Language.]

611. ———. "Aristotle's Syllogistic: A Medieval View." *Vivarium* 12 (1974): 18-29.
[Albert the Great. Aristotelianism: medieval. Syllogistic.]

612. Webb, Clement Charles Julian. *Ioannis Saresberiensis Episcopi Carnotensis Metalogicon Libri IIII.* Oxonii: E Typographeo Clarendoniano, 1929.
[John of Salisbury. Text.]

613. Webering, Damascene. *Theory of Demonstration according to William Ockham.* St. Bonaventure, N.Y.: The Franciscan Institute, Louvain: Éditions Nauwelaerts, Paderborn: F. Schöningh, 1953.
[Ockham. Demonstration.]

614. Weinberg, Julius Rudolph. "Historical Remarks on Some Medieval Views of Induction." In *Abstraction, Relation and Induction* by J. R. Weinberg, pp. 121-153. Madison and Milwaukee: The University of Wisconsin Press, 1965.
[Induction.]

615. Weisheipl, James A. "Roger Swyneshed, O.S.B., Logician, Natural Philosopher and Theologian." *Oxford Studies Presented to Daniel Callus. Oxford Historical Society* New Series (Oxford, 1964): 231-252.
[Swyneshed, Richard. Swyneshed, Roger.]

616. ———. "Curriculum of the Faculty of Arts at Oxford in the early Fourteenth Century." *Mediaeval Studies* 26 (1964): 143-185.
[Oxford.]

617. ———. "Developments in the Arts Curriculum at Oxford in the Early Fourteenth Century." *Mediaeval Studies* 28 (1966): 151-175.
[Oxford.]

618. ———. "Ockham and some Mertonians." *Mediaeval Studies* 30 (1968): 163-213.
[Bradwardine. Dumbleton. Heytesbury. Ockham. Swyneshed, Richard. Oxford.]

619. ———. "Repertorium Mertonense." *Mediaeval Studies* 31 (1969): 174-224.
[Billingham. Bradwardine. Burleigh. Dumbleton. Heytesbury. Richard of Campsall. Swyneshed, Richard. Manuscript sources. Oxford.]

620. ———. "The Liberal Arts in the xivth-xvth Century Curriculum." In *Arts libéraux et philosophie au moyen âge*, pp. 209-213. Montréal: Institut d'études médiévales, Paris: J. Vrin, 1969.
[Oxford. Paris.]

621. Werner, K. "Die Sprachlogik des Johannes Duns Scotus." *Sitzungsberichte der Philosophisch-historischen Classe der kaiserlichen Akademie der Wissenschaften.* Band 85 (Wien, 1877): 545-597.
[Duns Scotus. Thomas of Erfurt.]

622. Wielgus, S. and J. E. Zieliński. "Les questions sur les universaux de Benoît Hesse." *Mediaevalia Philosophica Polonorum* 14 (1970): 131-153.
[Hesse. Text. Universals.]

623. William, bishop of Lucca. Guglielmo. *Summa dialetice artis,* a cura e con introduzione di L. Pozzi. Padova, 1975. [Not seen.]
[William, bishop of Lucca. Text.]

624. William of Sherwood. *William of Sherwood's Introduction to Logic* translated with an introduction and notes by N. Kretzmann. Minneapolis: University of Minnesota Press, 1966.
[William of Sherwood. Translation.]
[Reviews: 265, 580.]

625. ———. *William of Sherwood's Treatise on Syncategorematic Words* translated with an introduction and notes by N. Kretzmann. Minneapolis: University of Minnesota Press, 1968.
[William of Sherwood. Translation. Syncategoremata.]
[Review: 229.]

626. Wilson, Curtis. *William Heytesbury. Medieval Logic and the Rise of Mathematical Physics.* Madison: The University of Wisconsin Press, 1956. Second Printing, 1960.
[Heytesbury. Sophisms.]

627. Włodek, Zofia. "Note sur l'inventaire des commentaires latins médiévaux sur les œuvres d'Aristote de Ch. H. Lohr." *Mediaevalia Philosophica Polonorum* 21 (1975): 153-154.
[Aristotle commentary.]
[Discussion of 288.]

628. Wójcik, Kazimierz. "Anonimowy wstęp do *Compendium logicae* Piotra ze Zgorzelca." *Roczniki Filozoficzne* 16 (1968): 139-146.
[Peter of Dresden. Text (anon.).]

629. Wycliffe, John. *Johannis Wyclif Tractatus de Logica. Now first edited from the Vienna and Prague mss. (Vienna 4352; Univ. Prag. v.e. 14)* by M. H. Dziewicki. 3 vol. London: Trübner & Co., 1893-1899.
[Wycliffe. Text.]

630. Yates, Frances A. "The Art of Ramon Lull. An Approach to it through Lull's Theory of the Elements." *Journal of the Warburg and Courtauld Institutes* 17 (1954): 115-173.
[Lull.]

631. Zadro, Attilio. "Nota per una ricerca sul concetto di logica di Pietro d'Abano." In *Atti del XII congresso internazionale di filosofia*, vol. 9, pp. 243-250. Firenze, 1960.
[Peter of Abano. Logic, concept of.]

632. Zimmermann, Albert. "Eine anonyme Quaestio: 'Utrum haec sit vera: "Homo est animal" homine non existente'." *Archiv für Geschichte der Philosophie* 49 (1967): 183-200.
[Text. Existential import.]

633. ——. "'Ipsum enim <"est"> nihil est' (Aristoteles, Periherm. I., c. 3). Thomas von Aquin über die Bedeutung der Kopula." In *Miscellanea Mediaevalia 8. Der Begriff der Repraesentatio im Mittelalter*, edited by A. Zimmermann, pp. 282-295. Berlin, New York: Walter de Gruyter & Co., 1971.
[Thomas Aquinas. Copula.]

Part Two

After Paul of Venice

634. Abranches, Cassiano. "Pedro da Fonseca. Valor e projecção da sua obra." *Revista portuguesa de filosofia* 16 (1960): 117-123.
    [Fonseca.]
    ——. See also Part One: 8.

635. Angelelli, Ignacio. "The Techniques of Disputation in the History of Logic." *The Journal of Philosophy* 67 (1970): 800-815.
    [Obligations.]
    ——. See also Part One: 16-17.

636. Antonaci, Antonio. "Il pensiero logico di Marcantonio Zimara (Ricerche sull'aristotelismo del Rinascimento)." In *Studi in onore di Antonio Corsano*, pp. 19-70. Manduria: Lacaita, 1970.
    [Zimara. Aristotelianism: Renaissance.]

637. ——. *Ricerche sull'Aristotelismo del Rinascimento. Marcantonio Zimara.* Volume 1: *Dal primo periodo padovano al periodo presalernitano.* Università di Bari pubblicazioni dell'Istituto di filosofia 14. Lecce-Galatina: Editrici Salentina, 1971.
    [Zimara. Aristotelianism: Renaissance.]

638. Argyropulos, Joannes. *Ioannis Argyropuli Dialectica ad Petrum de Medicis.* Edited by D. M. Inguanez and D. G. Muller. Miscellanea Cassinese, vol. 25. Montis Casini, 1943.
    [Argyropulos. George of Trebizond. Text.]
    [Discussion: 861.]

639. ——. Giovanni Argiropulo. "*Compendium de regulis et formis ratiocinandi* (Cod. Naz. Firenze II.11.52) con nota introduttiva di C. Vasoli." *Rinascimento* seconda serie 4 (1964): 285-339.
    [Argyropulos. Text.]

640. Ashworth, E. Jennifer. *The Logica Hamburgensis of Joachim Jungius*. Unpublished dissertation: Bryn Mawr College, 1964.
[Jungius.]

641. ———. "Joachim Jungius (1587-1657) and the Logic of Relations." *Archiv für Geschichte der Philosophie* 49 (1967): 72-85.
[Jungius. Relations.]

642. ———. "Propositional Logic in the Sixteenth and Early Seventeenth Centuries." *Notre Dame Journal of Formal Logic* 9 (1968): 179-192.
[Propositional logic.]
[Review: 855.]

643. ———. "Petrus Fonseca and Material Implication." *Notre Dame Journal of Formal Logic* 9 (1968): 227-228.
[Fonseca. Implication.]
[Review: 855.]

644. ———. "The Doctrine of Supposition in the Sixteenth and Seventeenth Centuries." *Archiv für Geschichte der Philosophie* 51 (1969): 260-285.
[Supposition.]

645. ———. "Some Notes on Syllogistic in the Sixteenth and Seventeenth Centuries." *Notre Dame Journal of Formal Logic* 11 (1970): 17-33.
[Syllogistic.]

646. ———. "The Treatment of Semantic Paradoxes from 1400 to 1700." *Notre Dame Journal of Formal Logic* 13 (1972): 34-52.
[Insolubilia.]

647. ———. "Strict and Material Implication in the Early Sixteenth Century." *Notre Dame Journal of Formal Logic* 13 (1972): 556-560.
[Implication.]

648. ———. "Are There Really Two Logics?" *Dialogue* 12 (1973): 100-109.
[Logic, history of.]

649. ———. "Existential Assumptions in Late Medieval Logic." *American Philosophical Quarterly* 10 (1973): 141-147.
[Existential import.]

650. ———. "Andreas Kesler and the Later Theory of Consequence." *Notre Dame Journal of Formal Logic* 14 (1973): 205-214.
[Kesler. Consequences.]

651. ——. "The Theory of Consequence in the Late Fifteenth and Early Sixteenth Centuries." *Notre Dame Journal of Formal Logic* 14 (1973): 289-315.
[Consequences.]

652. ——. "The Doctrine of Exponibilia in the Fifteenth and Sixteenth Centuries." *Vivarium* 11 (1973): 137-167.
[Exponibilia.]

653. ——. "Priority of Analysis and Merely Confused Supposition." *Franciscan Studies* 33 (1973): 38-41.
[Supposition.]
[Discussion of 560.]

654. ——. "Some Additions to Risse's *Bibliographia Logica*." *Journal of the History of Philosophy* 12 (1974): 361-365.
[Printed sources.]
[Discussion of 831.]

655. ——. "Classification Schemes and the History of Logic." In *Conceptual Basis of the Classification of Knowledge. Proceedings of the Ottawa Conference on the Conceptual Basis of the Classification of Knowledge, October 1st to 5th, 1971*, edited by J. A. Wojciechowski, pp. 275-283. Pullach-München: Verlag Dokumentation, 1974.
[Logic, history of.]

656. ——. "'For Riding is Required a Horse': A Problem of Meaning and Reference in Late Fifteenth and Early Sixteenth Century Logic." *Vivarium* 12 (1974): 94-123.
[Intentionality. Meaning. Reference.]

657. ——. *Language and Logic in the Post-Medieval Period*. Synthèse Historical Library 12. Dordrecht, Holland and Boston, U.S.A.: D. Reidel Publishing Company, 1974.
[Logic, history of.]
[Reviews: 840, 846.]

658. ——. "'I Promise You a Horse': A Second Problem of Meaning and Reference in Late Fifteenth and Early Sixteenth Century Logic (1)." *Vivarium* 14 (1976): 62-79. Continued: Ibid., 14 (1976): 139-155.
[Intentionality. Meaning. Reference.]

659. ——. "Agostino Nifo's Reinterpretation of Medieval Logic." *Rivista critica di storia della filosofia* 31 (1976): 355-374.
[Nifo.]

660. Baudry, Léon. *La querelle des futurs contingents. Louvain (1465-1475). Textes inédits.* Paris: J. Vrin, 1950.
[Text. Future contingents.]
———. See also Part One: 36.

661. Berka, K. and S. Sousedík. "On the Relational Logic of Ioannes Caramuel Lobkowiz." *Ruch Filozoficzny* 30 (1972): 50-52.
[Caramuel Lobkowitz. Relations.]

662. ———. "K Relační logice Jana Caramuela z Lobkovic." *Acta Universitatis Carolinae Philosophica et Historica* 2. *Studia Logica* (1972): 9-16.
[Caramuel Lobkowitz. Relations.]

663. Bocheński, Innocentius Maria. "Duae 'Consequentiae' Stephani de Monte." *Angelicum* 12 (1935): 397-399.
[Stephanus de Monte. Consequences.]
———. See also Part One: 55-63.

664. Boh, Ivan. "A 15th Century Systematization of Primary Logic." In *Memorias del XIII Congreso Internacional de Filosofía*, Volumen 5, pp. 47-57. Mexico: Universidad Nacional Autónoma de México, 1964.
[Paul of Pergula. Consequences.]

665. ———. "Paul of Pergula on Suppositions and Consequences." *Franciscan Studies* 25 (1965): 30-89.
[Paul of Pergula. Translation. Consequences.]

666. ———. "Propositional Connectives, Supposition and Consequence in Paul of Pergola." *Notre Dame Journal of Formal Logic* 7 (1966): 109-128.
[Paul of Pergula. Consequences. Supposition.]

667. ———. [Review of] V. Muñoz Delgado. *La lógica nominalista en la Universidad de Salamanca (1510-1530).* In *The New Scholasticism* 49 (1975): 377-382.
[Review of 769.]
———. See also Part One: 82-86.

668. Bonilla y San Martín, Adolfo and D. Marcelino Menéndez y Pelayo. *Fernando de Córdoba (¿1425-1486?) y los orígines del renacimiento filosófico en España. Episodio de la historia de la lógica.* Madrid: Librería general de Victoriano Suárez, 1911.
[Córdoba, Fernando de. Text.]

669. Bottin, Francesco. "La teoria del 'regressus' in Giacomo Zabarella." In *Saggi e ricerche su Aristotele, S. Bernardo, Zabarella, Miceli, Berger, Picasso, Wisdom, La propaganda, L'insegnamento della filosofia*, a cura di C. Giacon, pp. 49-70. Padova: Editrice Antenore, 1972.
[Zabarella.]

670. ———. "Nota sulla natura della logica in Giacomo Zabarella." *Giornale Critico della Filosofia Italiana* 4 (1973): 39-51.
[Zabarella. Logic, concept of.]
———. See also Part One: 88-93.

671. Burns, J. H. "New Light on John Major." *The Innes Review* 5 (1954): 83-100.
[Major.]

672. Caldi, Giuseppe. *La critica nel secolo XVI contro la logica aristotelica e l'insegnamento scolastico*. Udine: Jacob e Colmega, 1896. 33 pp.
[Not seen.]
[Humanism.]

673. Camporeale, Salvatore I. *Lorenzo Valla. Umanesimo e teologia*. Istituto Nazionale di Studi sul Rinascimento. Firenze: Nella Sede dell'Istituto Palazzo Strozzi, 1972.
[Valla, Lorenzo. Humanism.]

674. Carreras y Artau, Joaquín. *De Ramón Lull á los modernos. Ensayos de formación de una lengua universal. Lección inaugural....* Barcelona, 1946.
[Lull. Language.]

675. Ceñal, Ramón. "La historia de la lógica en España y Portugal de 1500 a 1800." *Pensamiento* 28 (1972): 277-319.
[Spain.]

676. Church, Alonzo. [Review of] F. C. Wade. Translator's Introduction. *John of St. Thomas. Outlines of Formal Logic*. In *The Journal of Symbolic Logic* 24 (1959): 81-83.
[Review of 742.]

677. ———. [Review of] Joachim Jungius. *Logica Hamburgensis*. In *The Journal of Symbolic Logic* 33 (1968): 139.
[Review of 744.]
———. See also Part One: 119.

678. Corsano, A. "Lo strumentalismo logico di I. Zabarella." *Giornale Critico della Filosofia Italiana* 16 (1962): 507-517.
[Zabarella. Method.]

679. Cranz, Ferdinand Edward. *A Bibliography of Aristotle Editions 1501-1600 with an introduction and indexes.* Bibliotheca Bibliographica Aureliana 38. Baden-Baden, 1971.
[Aristotle commentary. Printed sources.]

680. Crescini, Angelo. *Le origini del metodo analitico. Il cinquecento.* Udine: Del Bianco Editore, 1965.
[Italy. Method.]

681. ———. *Il problema metodologico alle origini della scienza moderna.* Roma: Edizioni dell'Ateneo, 1972.
[Italy. Method.]

682. Curtis, Mark H. "Library Catalogues and Tudor Oxford and Cambridge." *Studies in the Renaissance* 5 (1958): 111-120.
[Cambridge. Oxford.]

683. Dassonville, Michel. "La 'Dialectique' de Pierre de la Ramée, première œuvre philosophique originale en langue française." *La Revue de l'Université Laval* 7 (1952-1953): 608-616.
[Ramus.]

684. ———. "La genèse et les principes de la dialectique de Pierre de la Ramée." *Revue de l'Université d'Ottawa* 23 (1953): 322-355.
[Ramus.]

685. Del Cura, Alejandro. "Domingo de Soto, maestro de filosofía." *Estudios Filosóficos* 9 (1960): 391-440.
[Soto.]

686. Del Torre, Maria Assunta. *Studi su Cesare Cremonini. Cosmologia e logica nel tardo aristotelismo padovano.* Padova: Editrice Antenore, 1968.
[Cremonini. Aristotelianism: Renaissance. Padua.]

687. Dias, Arnaldo de Pinho. "A Isagoge de Porfírio na Lógica Conimbricense." *Revista Portuguesa de Filosofia* 20 (1964): 108-130.
[Aristotle commentary.]

688. Dionisotti, Carlo. "Ermolao Barbaro e la fortuna di Suiseth." In *Medioevo e Rinascimento. Studi in onore di B. Nardi.* Vol. 1, pp. 217-253. Firenze: G. C. Sansoni, 1955.
[Swyneshed, Richard. Italy.]

689. Doyle, John J. "John of St. Thomas and Mathematical Logic." *The New Scholasticism* 27 (1953): 3-38.
   [John of St. Thomas.]

690. Duhamel, Pierre Albert. "The Logic and Rhetoric of Peter Ramus." *Modern Philology* 46 (1948-1949): 163-171.
   [Ramus.]

691. ———. "Milton's Alleged Ramism." *Publications of the Modern Language Association of America* 67 (1952): 1035-1053.
   [Milton. Ramism.]

692. Durkan, John. "John Major: After 400 Years." *The Innes Review* 1 (1950): 131-139.
   [Major.]

693. ———. "The School of John Major—Bibliography." *The Innes Review* 1 (1950): 140-157.
   [Printed sources.]

694. ———. "George Lockhart." *The Innes Review* 15 (1964): 191-192.
   [Lockhart.]

695. Dürr, Karl. "Die Syllogistik des Johannes Hospinianus (1515-1575)." *Synthèse* 9 [no year] 472-484.
   [Hospinianus. Syllogistic.]
   ———. See also Part One: 145.

696. Edwards, William F. *The Logic of Iacopo Zabarella (1533-1589).* Unpublished dissertation: Columbia University, 1960. [Not seen.]
   [Zabarella.]

697. ———. "The Averroism of Iacopo Zabarella (1533-1589)." In *Atti del XII Congresso Internazionale di Filosofia*, vol. 9, pp. 91-107. Firenze, 1960.
   [Zabarella. Method.]

698. ———. "Randall on the Development of Scientific Method in the School of Padua—A Continuing Reappraisal." In *Naturalism and Historical Understanding. Essays on the Philosophy of John Herman Randall Jr.*, pp. 53-68. Buffalo: State University of New York Press, 1967.
   [Method. Padua.]

699. ———. "Jacopo Zabarella: A Renaissance Aristotelian's View of Rhetoric and Poetry and their Relation to Philosophy." In *Arts*

libéraux et philosophie au moyen âge, pp. 843-854. Montréal: Institut d'études médiévales, Paris: J. Vrin, 1969.
[Zabarella. Rhetoric.]

700. ———. "Niccolò Leoniceno and the Origins of Humanist Discussion of Method." In *Philosophy and Humanism. Renaissance Essays in Honor of Paul Oskar Kristeller*, edited by Edward P. Mahoney, pp. 283-305. Leiden: E. J. Brill, 1976.
[Leoniceno. Method.]

701. Elie, Hubert. "Quelques maîtres de l'université de Paris vers l'an 1500." *Archives d'histoire doctrinale et littéraire du moyen âge* 25e et 26e années (tome 18) (1950-1951): 193-243.
[Paris.]
———. See also Part One: 155.

702. Faggi, Adolfo. "Un trattato logico di Milton." *Atti e memorie della Reale Accademia di scienze, lettere ed arti in Padova*. Anno 373. Nuova serie. Volume 30 (1913-1914): 171-181.
[Milton.]

703. Faust, August. "Die Dialektik Rudolph Agricolas. Ein Beitrag zur Charakteristik des deutschen Humanismus." *Archiv für Geschichte der Philosophie* 34 (N.F. 27) (1922): 118-135.
[Agricola. Humanism.]

704. Fisher, Peter F. "Milton's Logic." *Journal of the History of Ideas* 23 (1962): 37-60.
[Milton.]

705. Fletcher, John M. *The Teaching and Study of Arts at Oxford, c. 1400 - c. 1520.* Unpublished dissertation: University of Oxford, 1962. [Not seen.]
[Oxford.]

706. Fonseca, Petrus. Pedro da Fonseca. *Instituições Dialécticas. Institutionum Dialecticarum libri Octo.* Introdução, estabelecimento do texto, tradução e notas por Joaquim Ferreira Gomes. 2 volumes. Coimbra: Universidade de Coimbra, 1964.
[Fonseca. Text. Translation.]

707. Franceschini, F. "Osservazioni sulla Logica di Jacopo Zabarella." *Società Italiana per il Progresso delle Scienze .... Atti della XXVI Riunione Venezia 12-18 Settembre 1937*. Volume 3º (Roma, 1938): 371-383.
[Zabarella.]

708. Gabriel, Astrik L. "'Via antiqua' and 'via moderna' and the Migration of Paris Students and Masters to the German Universities in the Fifteenth Century." In *Miscellanea Mediaevalia* 9. *Antiqui und Moderni. Traditionsbewusstsein und Fortschrittsbewusstsein im späten Mittelalter*, edited by A. Zimmermann, pp. 439-483. Berlin, New York: Walter de Gruyter, 1974.
[Germany. Nominalism.]

709. Garin, Eugenio. "Note su alcuni aspetti delle Retoriche rinascimentali e sulla 'Retorica' del Patrizi." *Testi Umanistici su la Retorica. Archivio di Filosofia* 3 (1953): 7-55.
[Rhetoric.]

710. ——. *Italian Humanism: Philosophy and Civic Life in the Renaissance*, translated by P. Munz. Oxford: Basil Blackwell, 1965.
[Humanism. Italy.]
——. See also Part One: 173-174.

711. Gerl, Hanna Barbara. *Rhetorik als Philosophie: Lorenzo Valla*. München: Wilhelm Fink Verlag, 1974.
[Valla, Lorenzo. Humanism. Rhetoric.]

712. Geulincx, Arnold. *Opera Philosophica*, edited by J. P. N. Land. 3 volumes. The Hague, 1891-1893.
[Geulincx. Text.]

713. Giacobbe, Giulio Cesare. "Il *Commentarium de certitudine mathematicarum disciplinarum* di Alessandro Piccolomini." *Physis* 14 (1972): 162-193.
[Piccolomini. Mathematics.]

714. ——. "Francesco Barozzi e la *Quaestio de certitudine mathematicarum.*" *Physis* 14 (1972): 357-374.
[Barozzi. Mathematics.]

715. ——. "Alcune cinquecentine riguardanti il processo di rivalutazione epistemologica della matematica nell'ambito della rivoluzione scientifica rinascimentale." *La Berio* [Bolletino bibliografico quadrimestrale] 13 (1973): 7-44. [Journal not seen.]
[Catena. Mathematics.]

716. ——. "La 'Quaestio de Certitudine Mathematicarum' all'interno della Scuola Padovana." In *Atti del Convegno di Storia della Logica (Parma 8-10 Ottobre 1972)*, pp. 203-212. Padova: Liviana Editrice, 1974.
[Mathematics. Padua.]

717. Gilbert, Neal Ward. *Renaissance Concepts of Method.* New York: Columbia University Press, 1960.
[Method.]

718. ——. "The Early Italian Humanists and Disputation." In *Renaissance Studies in Honor of Hans Baron*, edited by A. Molho and J. A. Tedeschi, pp. 201-226. Firenze: G. C. Sansoni Editore, 1971.
[Humanism. Italy.]

719. ——. "Ockham, Wyclif and the 'via moderna'." In *Miscellanea Mediaevalia 9. Antiqui und Moderni. Traditionsbewusstsein und Fortschrittsbewusstsein im späten Mittelalter*, edited by A. Zimmermann, pp. 85-125. Berlin, New York: Walter de Gruyter, 1974.
[Nominalism.]
——. See also Part One: 182.

720. Glanville, John J. "Zabarella and Poinsot on the Object and Nature of Logic." In *Readings in Logic*, edited by R. Houde, pp. 204-226. Dubuque, Iowa: William C. Brown Company, 1958.
[John of St. Thomas. Zabarella. Logic, concept of.]

721. Gomes, Joaquim Ferreira. "No quarto centenário das Instituições Dialécticas de Pedro da Fonseca." *Revista portuguesa de filosofia* 20 (1964): 273-292.
[Fonseca.]

722. ——. "Pedro da Fonseca: Sixteenth Century Portuguese Philosopher." *International Philosophical Quarterly* 6 (1966): 632-644.
[Fonseca.]

723. Heath, Terrence. "Logical Grammar, Grammatical Logic, and Humanism in Three German Universities." *Studies in the Renaissance* 18 (1971): 9-64.
[Germany. Grammar. Humanism.]

724. Herculano de Carvalho, José G. "Segno e significazione in João de São Tomás." In *Portugiesische Forschungen der Görresgesellschaft. Erste Reihe. Aufsätze zur portugiesischen Kulturgeschichte.* 2. Band, herausgegeben von Hans Flasche, pp. 152-176. Münster-Westfalen: Aschendorff, 1961.
[John of St. Thomas. Signification.]

725. Hickman, Larry. "Late Scholastic Logics: Another Look." *Journal of the History of Philosophy* 9 (1971): 226-234.
[Printed sources.]
[Discussion of 831.]

726. ——. [Review of] Wilhelm Risse. *Die Logik der Neuzeit.* In *Annals of Science* 32 (1975): 515-516.
[Review of 830.]
——. See also Part One: 236.

727. Himy, Armand. "La 'Logique' de Milton." *Revue Philosophique de la France et de l'Étranger* Tome 163, 98ᵉ année (1973): 155-170.
[Milton.]

728. Höltgen, Karl Josef. "Synoptische Tabellen in der medizinischen Literatur und die Logik Agricolas und Ramus'." In *Sudhoffs Archiv für Geschichte der Medizin und der Naturwissenschaften* herausgegeben von Edith Heischkel, Hans Schimank, Johannes Steudel, Rudolph Zaunick, Band 49, pp. 371-390. Wiesbaden: Franz Steiner Verlag GMBH, 1965.
[Agricola. Ramus.]

729. Hooykaas, R. *Humanisme, Science et Réforme. Pierre de la Ramée (1515-1572).* Leyde: E. J. Brill, 1958.
[Ramus.]

730. Hoorman, Cyril F. A. "A Further Examination of Saccheri's Use of the 'Consequentia Mirabilis'." *Notre Dame Journal of Formal Logic* 17 (1976): 239-247.
[Saccheri. Consequences.]

731. Howell, Wilbur Samuel. *Logic and Rhetoric in England, 1500-1700.* New York: Russell & Russell, Inc., 1956.
[England. Humanism. Rhetoric.]

732. Ijsewijn, Jozef. "Alexander Hegius (†1498) *Invectiva in Modos Significandi.*" *Forum for Modern Language Studies* 7 (1971): 299-318. Reprinted in *Renaissance Studies. Six Essays*, edited by I. D. McFarlane, A. H. Ashe, D. D. R. Owen, pp. 1-20. Edinburgh and London: Scottish Academic Press, 1972.
[Hegius. Text. Modi significandi.]

733. Jaeger, Henry-Evrard Hasso. "Studien zur Frühgeschichte der Hermeneutik." *Archiv für Begriffsgeschichte* 18 (1974): 35-84.
[Logic, history of.]

734. Jardine, Lisa. *Francis Bacon. Discovery and the Art of Discourse.* London-New York: Cambridge University Press, 1974.
[Bacon, Francis. Humanism.]

735. ——. "The Place of Dialectic Teaching in Sixteenth-Century Cambridge." *Studies in the Renaissance* 21 (1974): 31-62.
[Cambridge. Humanism.]

736. ——. "Humanism and the Sixteenth Century Cambridge Arts Course." *History of Education* 4 (1975): 16-31.
[Cambridge. Humanism.]

737. ——. "Humanism and Dialectic in Sixteenth-Century Cambridge: A Preliminary Investigation." In *Classical Influences on European Culture AD 1500-1700*, edited by R. R. Bolgar, pp. 141-154. Cambridge: Cambridge University Press, 1976.
[Cambridge. Humanism.]

738. Jardine, Nicholas. "Galileo's Road to Truth and the Demonstrative Regress." *Studies in the History and Philosophy of Science* 7 (1976): 277-318.
[Zabarella. Method.]

739. John of St. Thomas. *Ioannis a Sancto Thoma O.P. Cursus Philosophicus Thomisticus*. I. *Ars Logica seu De Forma et Materia Ratiocinandi*. Torino: Marietti, 1930.
[John of St. Thomas. Text.]

740. ——. "*Entia Rationis* and Second Intentions, Translated by John J. Glanville, G. Donald Hollenhorst, and Yves R. Simon." *The New Scholasticism* 23 (1949): 395-413.
[John of St. Thomas. Translation. Intentions.]

741. ——. *The Material Logic of John of St. Thomas. Basic Treatises* translated by Y. R. Simon, J. J. Glanville, G. D. Hollenhorst. Chicago: The University of Chicago Press, 1955.
[John of St. Thomas. Translation.]

742. ——. *Outlines of Formal Logic*. Translated from the Latin with an Introduction by F. C. Wade. Milwaukee, Wisc.: Marquette University Press, 1955.
[John of St. Thomas. Translation.]
[Review of Introduction: 676.]

743. John of Stobnica [Johannes Stobnicensis]. *Generalis doctrina de modis significandi grammaticalibus*. In *Metrificale Marka z Opatowca i Traktaty Gramatyczne XIV i XV Wieku* by Ryszard Gansiniec, pp. 149-154. Wrocław: Zakład Narodowy Imienia Ossolińskich Wydawnictwo Polskiej Akademii Nauk, 1960.
[John of Stobnica. Text. Modi significandi.]

744. Jungius, Joachim. *Joachimi Jungii Logica Hamburgensis*, edidit R. W. Meyer. In aedibus J. J. Augustin Hamburgi, 1957.
   [Jungius. Text. Translation.]
   [Review: 677.]

745. Kangro, Hans. "Joachim Jungius und Gottfried Wilhelm Leibniz. Ein Beitrag zum geistigen Verhältnis beider Gelehrten." *Studia Leibnitiana* 1 (1969): 175-207.
   [Jungius.]

746. Kenney, W. Henry. *John Locke and the Oxford Training in Logic and Metaphysics.* Unpublished dissertation: Saint Louis University, 1959.
   [Oxford.]

747. Korcik, Antoni. "O nowych formach sylogistycznych u J. C. Sturma." *Wydział Nauk Społecznych Polskiej Akademii Sprawozdania z prac naukowych wydziału nauk społecznych.* Rok 5, Zeszyt 4 (26) (1962) [printed 1963]: 50-55.
   [Sturm. Syllogistic.]
   ———. See also Part One: 270.

748. Kottman, Karl A. "Fray Luis de León and the Universality of Hebrew: An Aspect of 16th and 17th Century Language Theory." *Journal of the History of Philosophy* 13 (1975): 297-310.
   [León. Language.]

749. Kristeller, Paul Oskar. *Iter Italicum. A Finding List of Uncatalogued or Incompletely Catalogued Humanistic Manuscripts of the Renaissance in Italian and Other Libraries.* 1. *Italy. Agrigento to Novara.* London: The Warburg Institute, Leiden: E. J. Brill, 1963. 2. *Italy. Orvieto to Volterra. Vatican City.* London: The Warburg Institute, Leiden: E. J. Brill, 1967.
   [Manuscript sources.]

750. Lohr, Charles H. "Renaissance Latin Aristotle Commentaries: Authors A-B." *Studies in the Renaissance* 21 (1974): 228-289.
   [Manuscript sources. Printed sources.]
   ———. See also Part One: 287-296.

751. Loria, Gino. "La logique mathématique avant Leibniz." *Bulletin des sciences mathématiques* Deuxième série: Tome 18, Tome 28 de la collection (1894): 107-112.
   [Hérigone.]

752. McCain, John Walter, Jr. "Milton's *Artis Logicae.*" *Notes and Queries* 164 (1933): 149-150.
[Milton.]

753. Marco, Mario de. "La dottrina logica di I. Zabarella." *Bolletino di storia della filosofia* [Lecce] 1 (1973): 303-317.
[Zabarella.]

754. Margalho, Pedro. *Escólios em ambas as Lógicas à Doutrina de S. Tomás, do subtil Duns Escoto e dos nominalistas.* Reprodução facsimilada da edição de Salamanca, 1520. Tradução de Miguel Pinto de Meneses. Introdução pelo Professor Wilhelm Risse. Lisboa: Instituto de alta culture, 1965.
[Margalho. Text. Translation.]

755. Melanchthon, Philip. *Opera quae supersunt omnia*, edited by C. G. Bretschneider and [after Vol. 16] H. E. Bindseil. 28 volumes. Halle and Braunschwig, 1834-1860.
[Melanchthon. Text.]

756. Meurer, J. *Zur Logik des Heinrich Cornelius Agrippa von Nettesheim. Renaissance and Philosophie. Beiträge zur Geschichte der Philosophie*, herausgegeben von Dr. Adolf Dyroff. Heft 11. Bonn: Verlag von Peter Hanstein, 1920.
[Agrippa.]

757. Miller, Perry. *The New England Mind: The Seventeenth Century.* New York: Macmillan Co., 1939.
[Logic, history of.]

758. Monfasani, John. *George of Trebizond: A Biography and a Study of His Rhetoric and Logic.* Leiden: E. J. Brill, 1976.
[George of Trebizond. Rhetoric.]

759. Moore-Smith, G. C. "A Note on Milton's *Art of Logic.*" *The Review of English Studies* 13 (1937): 335-340.
[Milton.]

760. Moreno, Alberto. "Implicación material en Juan de Santo Tomás." *Sapientia* 14 (1959): 188-191.
[John of St. Thomas. Implication.]

761. ———. "Lógica proposicional en Juan de Santo Tomás." *Notre Dame Journal of Formal Logic* 4 (1963): 113-134. Also printed in *Sapientia* 18 (1963): 86-107.
[John of St. Thomas. Propositional logic.]

762. Muñoz Delgado, Vicente. "La enseñanza de la lógica en Salamanca durante el siglo XVI." *Salmanticensis* 1 (1954): 133-167.
[Salamanca.]

763. ———. "Domingo de Soto y la ordenación de la Enseñanza de la Lógica." *La Ciencia Tomista* [Salamanca] 87 (1960): 467-528.
[Journal not seen.]
[Soto.]

764. ———. "Las súmulas de lógica del curso de filosofía de Fray Pedro de Oña (1560-1626)." *Estudios* 17 (1961): 411-436.
[Oña.]

765. ———. "La exposición sumulista de la doctrina silogística de Fray Domingo de San Juan de Pie del Puerto (†1540)." *Estudios* 19 (1963): 3-49.
[San Juan de Pie del Puerto.]

766. ———. "Narciso Gregori y la lógica del humanismo en Salamanca durante la segunda mitad del siglo XVI." *Estudios* 19 (1963): 247-254.
[Gregori. Humanism. Salamanca.]

767. ———. "Reflexiones acerca de la naturaleza de la lógica en la obra de Domingo [de] Soto." *Estudios* 20 (1964): 3-45.
[Soto. Logic, concept of.]

768. ———. *Lógica formal y filosofía en Domingo de Soto (1494-1560)*. Madrid: Edita Revista "Estudios", 1964.
[Soto.]

769. ———. *La lógica nominalista en la Universidad de Salamanca (1510-1530)*. Madrid: Edita Revista "Estudios", 1964.
[Nominalism. Salamanca.]
[Review: 667.]

770. ———. "Confirmación de la interpretación anterior en la obra lógica de Domingo de Soto." *Estudios* 20 (1964): 179-216.
[Soto. Logic, concept of.]

771. ———. "Fray Narciso Gregori (1516-1561), médico, filosofo, y humanista." *Asclepio* 16 (1964): 193-203.
[Gregori.]

772. ———. "Domingo Báñez y las Súmulas en Salamanca a fines del siglo XVI." *Estudios* 21 (1965): 3-20.
[Báñez. Salamanca.]

773. ——. "Domingo de San Juan de Pie del Puerto y su obra lógica acerca de las 'Oppositiones' entre propositiones." *Estudios* 21 (1965): 161-186.
[San Juan de Pie del Puerto. Opposition.]

774. ——. "La lógica como 'scientia sermocinalis' en la obra de Pedro Sánchez Ciruelo (1470-1554)." *Estudios* 22 (1966): 23-52.
[Sánchez Ciruelo. Logic, concept of.]

775. ——. *La obra lógica de Pedro de la Serna*. Madrid: Edita Revista "Estudios", 1966.
[De la Serna.]

776. ——. "Los commentarios a la lógica de Aristóteles de José de San Marcelino." *Estudios* 22 (1966): 187-204.
[San Marcelino. Aristotle commentary.]

777. ——. "La lógica en Salamanca durante la primera mitad del siglo XVI." *Salmanticensis* 14 (1967): 171-207.
[Salamanca.]

778. ——. "Fuentes impresas de Lógica hispano-portuguesa del siglo XVI." In *Repertorio de Historia de las Ciencias Eclesiásticas en España* 1, pp. 435-464. Salamanca, 1967.
[Printed sources.]

779. ——. "La lógica en la Universidad de Alcalá durante la primera mitad del siglo XVI." *Salmanticensis* 15 (1968): 161-218.
[Alcalá.]

780. ——. "La obra lógica de los españoles en Paris (1500-1525)." *Estudios* 26 (1970): 209-280.
[Paris.]

781. ——. "El compendio de 'Dialéctica' (1633) de Martín Cajol; profesor de la Universidad de Huesca." *Estudios* 27 (1971): 207-235.
[Cajol.]

782. ——. "Cardillo de Villalpando y la lógica renacentista en Alcalá." *Estudios* 27 (1971): 511-555.
[Cardillo de Villalpando. Alcalá.]

783. ——. "Los 'Principia Dialectices' (1519) de Alonso de Córdoba." *La Ciudad de Dios* 185 (1972): 44-72.
[Córdoba, Alonso de.]

784. ——. *Lógica Hispano-Portuguesa hasta 1600 (Notas bibliográfico-doctrinales)*. Salamanca, 1972. Reprinted from: *Repertorio de historia de las ciencias eclesiasticas en España* 4 (1972): 9-122.
[Printed sources. Spain.]

785. ——. "La lógica de Bernardo Jordán. Estudio de su 'Explanatio in Petrum Hispanum' (Florencia, 1514)." *La Ciudad de Dios* 185 (1972): 439-462.
[Jordán.]

786. ——. "Pedro de Campis (c. 1498) y Juan Hidalgo (c. 1515). Dos médicos filósofos." *Cuadernos de Historia de la Medicina Española* 11 (1972): 359-371.
[Campis. Hidalgo.]

787. ——. "La 'Lógica' (1490) de Pedro de Castroval." *Antonianum* 48 (1973): 169-208.
[Castroval.]

788. ——. "Juan Hidalgo (1516) comentarista del 'Compendio de lógica' de Pablo de Venecia." *La Ciudad de Dios* 186 (1973): 20-36.
[Hidalgo.]

789. ——. "Lógica y filosofía en la naturaleza en un inédito de Francisco de Cristo (Coimbra 1556)." *La Ciudad de Dios* 186 (1973): 251-276.
[Cristo.]

790. ——. "España en la historia de la lógica prerrenacentista (1350-1550)." *La Ciudad de Dios* 186 (1973): 372-394.
[Spain.]

791. ——. "La lógica formal en España (1340-1540)." *Estudios* 29 (1973): 37-52.
[Spain.]

792. ——. "La filosofía entre los mercedarios del XVII y XVIII según unos inéditos de Palma." *Estudios* 29 (1973): 397-421.
[Spain.]

793. ——. "Luis de Lemos y su critica de la lógica humanistica." *Cuadernos de Historia de la Medicina Española* 12 (1973): 415-432.
[Lemos.]

794. ——. "La lógica renacentista en Pedro [Núñez] Vela, protestante abulense del XVI." *Dialogo Ecumenico* 9 (1974): 517-530.
   [Vela.]

795. ——. "Alonso de la Veracruz ante la reforma humanistica de la lógica." *La Ciudad de Dios* 187 (1974): 455-473.
   [De la Veracruz.]

796. ——. "Juan Aznar y su tratado de los términos (1513) según la via escotista." *Antonianum* 49 (1974): 304-319.
   [Aznar. Terms.]

797. ——. "Cipriano Benet y la lógica en el primer cuarto del siglo XVI." *Studium* 14 (1974): 131-144.
   [Benet.]

798. ——. "La obra lógica (1514) de Angel Estanyol." *Estudios filosóficos* 23 (1974): 69-89.
   [Stanyol, Angel.]
   ——. See also Part One: 366-369.

799. Nelson, Norman Edward. *Peter Ramus and the Confusion of Logic, Rhetoric and Poetry*. The University of Michigan Contributions in Modern Philology, No. 2. Ann Arbor: University of Michigan Press, 1947.
   [Ramus. Rhetoric.]

800. Ong, Walter Jackson. "Peter Ramus and the Naming of Methodism: Medieval Science Through Ramist Homiletic." *Journal of the History of Ideas* 14 (1953): 235-248.
   [Ramus. Ramism.]

801. ——. "Johannes Piscator: One Man or a Ramist Dichotomy?" *Harvard Library Bulletin* 8 (1954): 151-162.
   [Piscator.]

802. ——. *Ramus and Talon Inventory*. Cambridge, Mass.: Harvard University Press, 1958. Reprinted: Folcroft, Pa.: Folcroft Press, 1970.
   [Ramus. Printed sources.]

803. ——. *Ramus, Method and the Decay of Dialogue*. Cambridge, Mass.: Harvard University Press, 1958. Reprinted: New York: Octagon Books (Farrar, Strauss and Giroux), 1972.
   [Ramus.]

804. ——. "Ramist Method and the Commercial Mind." *Studies in the Renaissance* 8 (1961): 155-172.
[Ramism.]

805. ——. [Review of] Petrus Ramus. *Dialecticae Institutiones; Aristotelicae Animadversiones* (Facsimile Neudruck der Ausgaben Paris 1543, mit einer Einleitung von Wilhelm Risse, Stuttgart-Bad Cannstatt: Friedrich Frommann Verlag Günther Holzboog, 1964.) In *Renaissance News* 18 (1965): 31-33.
[Ramus.]

806. ——. [Review of] Pierre de la Ramée. *Dialectique (1555)*, edited by Michel Dassonville. In *Renaissance News* 19 (1966): 142-144.
[Review of 816.]

807. ——. [Review of] Peter Ramus. *The Logike of the Moste Excellent Philosopher P. Ramus Martyr.* Translated by Roland MacIlmaine (1574). Edited by Catherine M. Dunn. In *Renaissance Quarterly* 24 (1971): 87-90.
[Review of 817.]

808. ——. "Christianus Ursitius and Ramus' New Mathematics." *Bibliothèque d'Humanisme et Renaissance. Travaux et Documents* 36 (1974): 603-610.
[Ramus. Ursitius. Mathematics.]

809. Papuli, Giovanni. *Girolamo Balduino. Ricerche sulla logica della Scuola di Padova nel Rinascimento.* Università di Bari, Pubblicazioni dell'Istituto di Filosofia 12. Bari: Lacaita Editore, 1967.
[Balduino. Padua.]

810. ——. "B. Varchi: logica e poetica." In *Studi in onore di Antonio Corsano*, pp. 525-552. Manduria: Lacaita, 1970.
[Varchi.]

811. Pastore, Annibale. "G. Caramuel di Lobkowitz e la teoria della quantificazione del predicato." *Rivista Classici e Neolatini* (Aosta, 1905). [Not seen.]
[Caramuel Lobkowitz.]

812. Paul of Pergula. *Logica and Tractatus de Sensu Composito et Diviso.* Edited by Sister Mary Anthony Brown. St. Bonaventure, N.Y., Louvain, Paderborn: The Franciscan Institute, 1961.
[Paul of Pergula. Text. Composition and division.]

813. Pineas, Rainer. "John Frith's Polemical Use of Rhetoric and Logic." *Studies in English Literature 1500-1900* 4 (1964): 85-100.
[Frith. Rhetoric.]

814. Poppi, Antonino. "La natura della logica negli Scotisti Padovani del seicento." In *Storia e Cultura al Santo* a cura di Antonio Poppi, pp. 539-546. Vicenza: Neri Pozza Editore, 1976.
[Padua.]

815. Prieto del Rey, Maurilio. "Significación y sentido ultimado. La noción de 'suppositio' en la lógica de Juan de Santo Tomás." *Convivium* [Barcelona] Núm. 15-16 (1963): 33-73. Continued: Ibid., Núm. 19-20 (1965): 45-72.
[John of St. Thomas. Signification. Supposition.]

816. Ramus, Petrus. La Ramée, Pierre de. *Dialectique (1555)*. Édition critique, avec introduction, notes et commentaires de Michel Dassonville. Genève: Librairie Droz, 1964.
[Ramus. Text.]
[Review: 806.]

817. ———. *The Logike of the Moste Excellent Philosopher P. Ramus Martyr*. Translated by Roland MacIlmaine (1574). Edited by Catherine M. Dunn. San Fernando Valley State College, Northridge, California, 1969.
[Ramus. Translation.]
[Review: 807.]

818. Randall, John Herman, Jr. "The Development of Scientific Method in the School of Padua." *Journal of the History of Ideas* 1 (1940): 177-206.
[Method. Padua.]
[Reprinted: 820.]

819. ———. "Padua Aristotelianism: An Appraisal." In *Atti del XII Congresso Internazionale di Filosofia*, vol. 9, pp. 199-206. Firenze, 1960.
[Aristotelianism: Renaissance. Padua.]

820. ———. *The School of Padua and the Emergence of Modern Science*. Padova: Editrice Antenore, 1961.
[Method. Padua.]
[Includes reprint of 818.]

821. ———. "Paduan Aristotelianism Reconsidered." In *Philosophy and Humanism. Renaissance Essays in Honor of Paul Oskar Kristeller*,

edited by Edward P. Mahoney, pp. 275-282. Leiden: E. J. Brill, 1976.
[Aristotelianism: Renaissance. Padua.]

822. Renaudet, Augustin. *Préréforme et Humanisme à Paris pendant les premières guerres d'Italie (1494-1517)*. Paris, 1916. Deuxième édition, revue et corrigée. Paris: Librairie d'Argences, 1953.
[Paris.]

823. ———. "L'humanisme et l'enseignement de l'université de Paris au temps de la renaissance." In *Aspects de l'Université de Paris*, by L. Halphen et al., pp. 135-155. Paris: Éditions Albin Michel, 1949.
[Humanism. Paris.]

824. Rice, Eugene Franklin. "Humanist Aristotelianism in France. Jacques Lefèvre d'Étaples and his circle." In *Humanism in France at the End of the Middle Ages and in the Early Renaissance*, edited by A. H. T. Levi, pp. 132-149. Manchester: Manchester University Press, New York: Barnes & Noble, Inc., 1970.
[Le Fèvre d'Étaples. Aristotelianism: Renaissance. Humanism.]

825. Riley, Lyman Walter. *Aristotle Texts and Commentaries to 1700 in the University of Pennsylvania Library, a catalogue*. Philadelphia, 1961.
[Aristotle commentary. Printed sources.]

826. Risse, Wilhelm. "Die Entwicklung der Dialektik bei Petrus Ramus." *Archiv für Geschichte der Philosophie* 42 (1960): 36-72.
[Ramus.]

827. ———. "Mathematik und Kombinatorik in der Logik der Renaissance." *Archiv für Philosophie* 11 (1962): 187-206.
[Combinatorics. Mathematics.]

828. ———. "Zur Vorgeschichte der cartesischen Methodenlehre." *Archiv für Geschichte der Philosophie* 45 (1963): 269-291.
[Method.]

829. ———. "Averroismo e Alessandrinismo nella logica del rinascimento." *Filosofia* 15 (1964): 15-30.
[Averroism. Italy.]

830. ———. *Die Logik der Neuzeit*. I. Band. *1500-1640*. Stuttgart-Bad Cannstatt: Friedrich Frommann Verlag (Günther Holzboog), 1964.
[Logic, history of.]
[Review: 726.]

831. ——. *Bibliographia Logica. Verzeichnis der Druckschriften zur Logik mit Angabe ihrer Fundorte.* Band I. *1472-1800.* Hildesheim: Georg Olms Verlagsbuchhandlung, 1965.
[Printed sources.]
[Discussions: 654, 725.]

832. Rossi, Paolo. "Ramismo, logica, retorica nei secoli XVI e XVII." *Rivista critica di storia della filosofia* 12 (1957): 357-365.
[Ramus. Rhetoric.]

833. ——. "Enciclopedismo e combinatoria nel secolo XVI." *Rivista critica di storia della filosofia* 13 (1958): 243-279.
[Lull.]
[Partial translation: 836.]

834. ——. "Studi sul lullismo e sull'arte della memoria nel Rinascimento. IV. La memoria artificiale come sezione della logica: Ramo, Bacone, Cartesio." *Rivista critica di storia della filosofia* 15 (1960): 22-62.
[Bacon, Francis. Ramus. Lullism.]

835. ——. *Clavis Universalis. Arti mnemoniche e logica combinatoria da Lullo a Leibniz.* Milano-Napoli: Riccardo Ricciardi Editore, 1960.
[Lull. Combinatorics. Lullism.]

836. ——. "The Legacy of Ramon Lull in Sixteenth Century Thought." *Mediaeval and Renaissance Studies*, edited by Richard Hunt, Raymond Klibansky, Lotte Labowsky, 5 (1961): 182-213.
[Lull.]
[Partial translation of 833.]

837. Roure, M. L. "Le traité 'Des propositions insolubles' de Jean de Celaya." *Archives d'histoire doctrinale et littéraire du moyen âge* 29 (1962): 235-338.
[Celaya. Text. Translation. Insolubilia.]
——. See also Part One: 514.

838. Salmon, Vivian. [Review of] N. Chomsky. *Cartesian Linguistics.* In *Journal of Linguistics* 5 (1969): 165-187.
[Speculative grammar.]

839. Schmitt, Charles B. *A Critical Survey and Bibliography of Studies on Renaissance Aristotelianism 1958-1969.* Padova: Editrice Antenore, 1971.
[Aristotelianism: Renaissance.]

840. ——. [Review of] E. J. Ashworth. *Language and Logic in the Post-Medieval Period.* In *Annals of Science* 32 (1975): 516-517.
[Review of 657.]

841. ——. "Philosophy and Science in Sixteenth-Century Universities: Some Preliminary Comments." In *The Cultural Context of Medieval Learning*, edited by J. E. Murdoch and E. D. Sylla, pp. 485-537. Dordrecht, Holland and Boston, U.S.A.: D. Reidel Publishing Company, 1975.
[Aristotelianism: Renaissance. Italy. Oxford.]

842. Schüling, Hermann. *Bibliographie der im 17. Jahrhundert in Deutschland erschienenen logischen Schriften. Berichte und Arbeiten aus der Universitätsbibliothek Giessen.* 3. Giessen: Universitätsbibliothek, 1963.
[Germany. Printed sources.]

843. ——. *Die Geschichte der axiomatischen Methode im 16. und beginnenden 17. Jahrhundert.* Hildesheim, New York: Georg Olms, 1969.
[Axiomatic method. Mathematics. Syllogistic.]

844. Silvestro da Valsanzibio, O.F.M.Cap. *Vita e dottrina di Gaetano di Thiene, filosofo dello studio di Padova, 1387-1465.* 2a edizione. Padova: Studio Filosofico dei Fratrum Minorum Cappuccini, 1949.
[Cajetan of Thiene. Padua.]

845. Sousedík, Stanislav. "Diskrétni logika Jana Caramuela z Lobkovic." *Filosoficky časopis* 16 (1969): 216-228.
[Caramuel Lobkowitz. Relations.]

846. Spade, Paul Vincent. [Review of] E. J. Ashworth. *Language and Logic in the Post-Medieval Period.* In *Dialogue* 15 (1976): 333-340.
[Review of 657.]
——. See also Part One: 543-554.

847. Swieżawski, Stefan. "Matériaux servants aux recherches sur Jean de Glogów († 1507)." In *Mélanges offerts à Étienne Gilson de l'Académie Française*, pp. 613-650. Toronto: Pontifical Institute of Mediaeval Studies, Paris: J. Vrin, 1959.
[John of Glogovia.]
——. See also Part One: 559.

848. Thomas, Ivo. "Material Implication in John of St. Thomas." *Dominican Studies* 3 (1950): 180.
[John of St. Thomas. Implication.]

849. ——. "The Setting of Classical Logic." *The Scholastic* [Notre Dame] 101 (1960): 16-17. [Journal not seen.]
[Logic, history of.]

850. ——. "Medieval Aftermath: Oxford Logic and Logicians of the Seventeenth Century." *Oxford Studies Presented to Daniel Callus. Oxford Historical Society.* New Series 16 (Oxford, 1964): 297-311.
[Oxford.]

851. ——. "The Written Liar and Thomas Oliver." *Notre Dame Journal of Formal Logic* 6 (1965): 201-208.
[Oliver. Insolubilia.]

852. ——. "The Later History of the *Pons Asinorum*." In *Contributions to Logic and Methodology in Honor of J. M. Bocheński*, edited by A. T. Tymieniecka in collaboration with C. Parsons, pp. 142-150. Amsterdam: North-Holland Publishing Company, 1965.
[Pons asinorum.]

853. ——. "Interregnum" under "Logic, History of." In *The Encyclopedia of Philosophy*, edited by P. Edwards, vol. 4, pp. 534-537. New York-London: Macmillan & Free Press, 1967.
[Logic, history of.]
——. See also Part One: 576-580.

854. Trentman, John A. "The Study of Logic and Language in England in the Early 17th Century." *Historiographia Linguistica* 3 (1976): 179-201.
[Aristotelianism: Renaissance. England.]
——. See also Part One: 586-594.

855. Tweedale, Martin. [Reviews of] E. J. Ashworth. "Propositional Logic in the Sixteenth and Early Seventeenth Centuries." E. J. Ashworth. "Petrus Fonseca and Material Implication." In *The Journal of Symbolic Logic* 36 (1971): 323-324.
[Reviews of 642, 643.]
——. See also Part One: 596-599.

856. Uedelhofen, Matthias. *Die Logik Petrus Fonsecas. Renaissance und Philosophie. Beiträge zur Geschichte der Philosophie.* Herausgegeben von Adolf Dyroff. Heft 13. Bonn: Verlag von Peter Hanstein, 1916.
[Fonseca.]

857. Vasoli, Cesare. "Retorica e dialettica in Pietro Ramo." *Testi Umanistici su la retorica. Archivio di filosofia* 3 (1953): 93-134.
[Ramus. Rhetoric.]

858. ———. "Il Poliziano maestro di dialettica." In *Il Poliziano e il suo tempo. Atti del IV Convegno Internazionale di Studi sul Rinascimento*, pp. 161-172. Firenze: G. C. Sansoni, 1957.
[Politian. Humanism.]

859. ———. "Dialettica e Retorica in Rodolfo Agricola." *Atti e memorie dell'Accademia toscana di scienze e lettere 'La Colombaria'* 22 (NS 8) (1957): 305-355.
[Agricola. Rhetoric.]

860. ———. "Le 'Dialecticae Disputationes' del Valla e la critica umanistica della logica aristotelica I." *Rivista critica di storia della filosofia* 12 (1957): 412-434. II.: Ibid., 13 (1958): 27-46.
[Valla, Lorenzo. Humanism.]

861. ———. "Su una *Dialectica* attribuita all'Argiropulo." *Rinascimento* Anno 10 (1959): 157-164.
[Argyropulos. George of Trebizond.]
[Discussion of 638.]

862. ———. "Jacques Lefèvre d'Étaples e le origini del 'fabrismo'." *Rinascimento* Anno 10 (1959): 221-254.
[Le Fèvre d'Étaples. Humanism.]

863. ———. "La *dialectica* di Giorgio Trapezunzio." *Atti e memorie dell'Accademia toscana di scienze e lettere 'La Colombaria'* 24 (NS 10) (1959-1960): 299-327.
[George of Trebizond.]

864. ———. "Ricerche sulle 'Dialettiche' quattrocentesche." *Rivista critica di storia della filosofia* 15 (1960): 265-287.
[Argyropulos. Valla, Giorgio.]

865. ———. "Juan Luis Vives e un programma umanistico di riforma della logica." *Atti e memorie dell'Accademia toscana di scienze e lettere 'La Colombaria'* 25 (NS 11) (1960-1961): 217-263.
[Vives. Humanism.]

866. ———. "Giovanni Ludovico Vives e la polemica antiscolastica nello 'In pseudodialecticos'." *Miscelânea de Estudos a Joaquim de Carvalho* 7 (1961): 679-687.
[Vives. Humanism.]

867. ———. "Problemi e discussioni logiche nel cinquecento italiano." *Annali delle Facoltà di lettere, filosofia e magistero dell'università di Cagliari* 29 (1961-1965): 301-388.
[Humanism. Italy.]

868. ——. "Ricerche sulle 'Dialettiche' del cinquecento. I. L'influenza di Rodolfo Agricola e gli scritti dialettici del Latomus e del Caesarius." *Rivista critica di storia della filosofia* 20 (1965): 115-150.
[Agricola. Humanism.]

869. ——. "Ricerche sulle 'Dialettiche' del cinquecento. II. L'insegnamento logico del Melantone." *Rivista critica di storia della filosofia* 20 (1965): 451-480.
[Melanchthon.]

870. ——. "Ricerche sulle 'Dialettiche' del cinquecento. III. Sturm, Melantone e il problema del 'Metodo'." *Rivista critica di storia della filosofia* 21 (1966): 123-140.
[Melanchthon. Sturm. Method.]

871. ——. *La dialettica e la retorica dell'Umanesimo. 'Invenzione' e 'Metodo' nella cultura del XV e XVI secolo.* Milano: Feltrinelli, 1968.
[Humanism. Method. Rhetoric.]

872. ——. *Profezia e ragione. Studi sulla cultura del Cinquecento e del Seicento.* Napoli: Morano Editore, 1974.
[Humanism.]

873. ——. "La Logica Europea nell'Età dell'Umanesimo e del Rinscimento." In *Atti del Convegno di Storia della Logica (Parma 8-10 Ottobre 1972)*, pp. 61-94. Padova: Liviana Editrice, 1974.
[Humanism.]

——. See also Part One: 600-602.

874. Victor, Joseph M. "The Revival of Lullism at Paris, 1499-1516." *Renaissance Quarterly* 28 (1975): 504-534.
[Le Fèvre d'Étaples. Lull. Paris.]

875. Villoslada, Ricardo García. *La universidad de París durante los estudios de Francisco de Vitoria O.P., 1507-1522. Analecta Gregoriana* 14. Romae, 1938.
[Paris.]

876. Waddington-Kastus, Charles. *De Petri Rami Vita, Scriptis, Philosophia.* Parisiis: Apud Joubert, Bibliopolam, 1848.
[Ramus.]

877. ——. *Ramus (Pierre de la Ramée). Sa vie, ses écrits et ses opinions.* Paris: Librarie de Ch. Meyrueis et Cie, éditeurs, 1855.
[Ramus.]

878. Walton, Craig. "Ramus and Bacon on Method." *Journal of the History of Philosophy* 9 (1971): 289-302.
[Bacon, Francis. Ramus. Method.]

879. Wilson, Thomas. *The Rule of Reason Conteinying the Arte of Logique*. Edited by Richard S. Sprague. Northridge, Calif.: San Fernando Valley State College, 1972.
[Wilson. Text.]

880. Zippel, Giuseppe. "Note sulle redazioni della 'Dialectica' di Lorenzo Valla." *Archivio storico per le province parmensi* 9 (1957): 301-315.
[Valla, Lorenzo.]

Index of Names

References to authors outside the period covered by the bibliography will be found in the Index of Subjects.

Abelard, Peter 1, 2, 3, 4, 5, 6, 7, 40, 41, 42, 43, 44, 45, 46, 47, 48, 49, 114, 123, 131, 145, 196, 255, 257, 283, 336, 337, 338, 347, 373, 479, 530, 596, 599
Adam of Balsham 345, 346, 579
Agricola, Rudolph 703, 728, 859, 868
Agrippa, Heinrich Cornelius 756
Albert of Saxony 188
Albert the Great 11, 54, 210, 341, 522, 610, 611
Alfarabi 522
Algazel 287, 289, 515
Anselm 126, 220, 221, 222, 223, 224, 227, 228, 231, 233, 302, 490, 523
Argyropulos, Joannes 638, 639, 861, 864
Avicenna 187, 461, 536
Aznar, Juan 796

Bacon, Francis 734, 834, 878
Bacon, Roger 30, 31, 298
Balduino, Girolamo 809
Báñez, Domingo 772
Barozzi, Francesco 714
Benet, Cipriano 797
Billingham, Richard 311, 478, 481, 482, 619
Boethius of Dacia 80, 81, 96, 110, 154, 190, 197, 256, 505, 506
Bradlay, Peter 565, 566
Bradwardine, Thomas 514, 618, 619
Buridan, John 87, 103, 104, 152, 158, 159, 167, 177, 208, 235, 240, 241, 314, 321, 322, 323, 328, 355, 400, 430, 451, 453, 456, 457, 458, 459, 483, 492, 495, 531, 607
Burleigh, Walter 35, 82, 83, 84, 86, 98, 99, 100, 105, 206, 330, 392, 409, 450, 514, 535, 552, 606, 619

Cajetan, Thomas de Vio 20
Cajetan of Thiene 844
Cajol, Martin 781
Campis, Pedro de 786
Caramuel Lobkowitz, Johannes 661, 662, 811, 845
Cardillo de Villalpando, Gaspar 782
Castroval, Pedro de 787
Catena, Petrus 715
Celaya, Juan de 837
Chatton, Walter 168, 269
Córdoba, Alonso de 783
Córdoba, Fernando de 668
Crathorn 239, 526, 527, 528
Cremonini, Cesare 686
Cristo, Francisco de 789

Dante 18, 115
De la Serna, Pedro 775
De la Veracruz, Alonso 795
Dumbleton, John 618, 619
Duns Scotus, John 124, 144, 189, 217, 218, 219, 254, 442, 559, 585, 621

Eymerich, Nicholas 368

Fland, Robert 554
Fonseca, Pedro da 634, 643, 706, 721, 722, 856
Frith, John 813

Garlandus Compotista 175, 234
Gaunilon 128
George of Trebizond 638, 758, 861, 863
Gerland of Besançon 121
Geulincx, Arnold 712
Gilbert of Poitiers 216, 374
Giles of Rome 386, 491
Godfrey of Fontaines 96

Gregori, Narciso 766, 771
Gregory of Rimini 130, 171, 239, 391

Hegius, Alexander 732
Henry of Werla 120
Hérigone, Pierre 751
Hervaeus Natalis 425
Hesse, Benoît 622
Heytesbury, William 309, 310, 553, 618, 619, 626
Hidalgo, Juan 786, 788
Holkot, Robert 122, 129, 237, 239, 354, 363, 526, 527, 528
Hospinianus, Johannes 695
Hugh of St. Victor 202

Jacob of Placentia 278
Johannes Dacus 252, 389
Johannes Wuel 29
John of Glogovia 847
John of Grotkow 136
John of St. Thomas 119, 689, 720, 724, 739, 740, 741, 742, 760, 761, 815, 848
John of Salisbury 28, 172, 253, 393, 612
John of Stobnica 743
Jordán, Bernardo 785
Jordan of Saxony 203
Jungius, Joachim 640, 641, 744, 745

Kesler, Andreas 650
Kilmington, Richard 88, 89, 90
Kilwardby, Robert 261, 270, 577, 578, 581

Lambert of Auxerre 179, 281
Lavenham, Richard 544, 547, 550
Le Fèvre d'Étaples, Jacques 344, 824, 862, 874
Lemos, Luis de 793
Léon, Luis de 748
Leoniceno, Niccolò 700
Lockhart, George 694
Lull, Ramon 169, 271, 289, 291, 292, 433, 434, 435, 455, 515, 630, 674, 833, 835, 836, 874

Major, John 671, 692
Margalho, Pedro 754
Marsilius of Inghen 87, 484

Martin of Dacia 280, 331, 332, 372, 501, 503, 507
Matthew of Eugubio 277
Melanchthon, Philip 755, 869, 870
Milton, John 691, 702, 704, 727, 752, 759

Nicholas of Paris 192
Nifo, Agostino 659

Ockham, William 9, 10, 14, 15, 35, 36, 51, 64, 65, 66, 67, 68, 69, 70, 71, 72, 74, 75, 77, 79, 85, 98, 111, 112, 113, 119, 124, 168, 180, 226, 262, 284, 303, 308, 334, 335, 352, 365, 376, 377, 378, 379, 380, 381, 382, 383, 431, 447, 518, 519, 521, 525, 546, 548, 549, 552, 560, 593, 595, 600, 606, 613, 618
Odon, Gerard 101
Oliver, Thomas 851
Oña, Pedro de 764

Paul of Pergula 664, 665, 666, 812
Paul of Venice 63, 294, 391, 398
Peter Aureol 425
Peter Lombard 215
Peter of Abano 631
Peter of Ailly 142
Peter of Alverna 418, 423, 426
Peter of Dresden 628
Peter of Mantua 250, 313, 601
Peter of Spain 8, 94, 115, 162, 179, 303, 364, 401, 402, 403, 432, 437, 439, 448, 472, 473, 475, 511, 523, 540, 555, 582
Petrus Helias 164, 165, 242, 404, 523
Petrus Hispanus (Grammarian) 245
Piccolomini, Alessandro 713
Piscator, Johannes 801
Politian 858

Radulphus Brito 416, 419, 422, 425, 429
Ramus, Petrus 270, 271, 683, 684, 690, 728, 729, 799, 800, 802, 803, 805, 808, 816, 817, 826, 832, 834, 857, 876, 877, 878
Richard of Campsall 465, 561, 562, 563, 619
Roger of Nottingham 564

Saccheri, Gerolamo 730
Sánchez Ciruelo, Pedro 774
San Juan de Pie del Puerto, Domingo de 765, 773
San Marcelino, José de 776
Ps.-Scotus 39, 116, 304, 333, 340, 367
Siger of Brabant 32, 37, 181, 190, 319
Siger of Courtrai 407, 523, 537, 605, 609
Simon of Dacia 405, 538
Simon of Faversham 149, 389, 539
Soto, Domingo de 685, 763, 767, 768, 770
Stanyol, Angel 798
Stephanus de Monte 633
Stephanus de Reate 135
Stephen of Palecz 394
Strode, Ralph 533
Sturm, Johannes 747, 870
Sutton, Thomas 534
Swyneshed, Richard 615, 618, 619, 688
Swyneshed, Roger 615

Thierry of Chartres 163
Thomas Aquinas 13, 20, 58, 125, 132, 248, 279, 305, 315, 316, 317, 320, 351, 500, 512, 529, 567, 568, 569, 570, 571, 572, 573, 603, 604, 633
Thomas of Erfurt 102, 184, 185, 189, 198, 217, 218, 219, 259, 557, 574, 575, 621

Ursitius, Christianus 808

Valla, Giorgio 864
Valla, Lorenzo 673, 711, 860, 880
Varchi, B. 810
Vela, Pedro 794
Vincent Ferrer 348, 436, 576, 587, 590, 592, 608
Vives, Juan Luis 865, 866

William, bishop of Lucca 623
William of Champeaux 166, 209
William of Conches 164, 251
William of Moerbeke 13, 19, 22, 24, 26, 344, 541
William of Sherwood 194, 205, 206, 247, 318, 384, 477, 489, 514, 542, 624, 625
Wilson, Thomas 879
Wycliffe, John 629

Zabarella, Giacomo 669, 670, 678, 696, 697, 699, 707, 720, 738, 753
Zimara, Marcantonio 636, 637

Index of Texts

Abelard, Peter 1, 2, 3, 4, 5, 6, 7, 123, 347
Anonymous: Aristotle commentary 146, 147, 148, 151
  Existential import 632
  Fallacies 469
  Future contingents 660
  Grammar 583
  Insolubilia 95, 468, 543
  Intentions 137
  Obligations 477
  Paralogisms 153
  (Peter of Dresden) 628
  Supposition 471
  Universals 199
Aristotle: Latin 19, 21, 22, 23, 24, 25, 26
Adam of Balsham 346
Albert the Great 11, 54
Algazel 287
Anselm 227, 233
Argyropulus, Joannes 638, 639

Bacon, Roger 30, 31
Billingham, Richard 311, 478, 481
Boethius of Dacia 80, 81, 197, 505
Bradlay, Peter 565, 566
Bradwardine, Thomas 514
Buridan, John 103, 152, 208, 241, 430
Burleigh, Walter 84, 98, 99, 100, 105, 206, 392, 514, 535

Celaya, Juan de 837
Chatton, Walter 168
Córdoba, Fernando de 668

Duns Scotus, John 144

Fland, Robert 554
Fonseca, Pedro da 706

Garlandus Compotista 175
George of Trebizond 638
Geulincx, Arnold 712
Godfrey of Fontaines 96

Hegius, Alexander 732
Henry of Werla 120
Hesse, Benoît 622
Holkot, Robert 122, 363
Hugh of St. Victor 282

Johannes Dacus 252
Johannes Wuel 29
John of Grotkow 136
John of St. Thomas 739
John of Salisbury 612
John of Stobnica, 743
Jungius, Joachim 744

Kilwardby, Robert 261, 577

Lambert of Auxerre 281
Lavenham, Richard 544, 547
Lull, Ramon 289, 515

Margalho, Pedro 754
Martin of Dacia 331, 332
Melanchthon, Philip 755

Ockham, William 67, 111, 112, 113, 376, 377, 378, 379, 383
Odon, Gerard 101

Paul of Pergula 812
Paul of Venice 398
Peter of Alvernia 423
Peter of Spain 364, 401, 403

Radulphus Brito 429
Ramus, Petrus 816
Richard of Campsall 465, 561, 562, 563
Roger of Nottingham 564

Siger of Brabant 32, 37, 319
Siger of Courtrai 407, 537, 609
Simon of Dacia 538
Simon of Faversham 389, 539
Stephanus de Reate 135

Stephen of Palecz 394
Strode, Ralph 533

Themistius (Latin) 385
Thomas Aquinas 58, 500, 567, 568, 569, 570, 572, 604
Thomas of Erfurt 574, 575

Vincent Ferrer 608

William, bishop of Lucca 623
William of Conches 251
William of Moerbeke 541
William of Sherwood 194, 206, 384, 477, 514
Wilson, Thomas 879
Wycliffe, John 629

Index of Translations

Anselm 227, 233
Avicenna 536

Buridan, John 104
Burleigh, Walter 84

Cajetan, Thomas de Vio 20
Celaya, Juan de 837

Fonseca, Pedro da 706

John of St. Thomas 740, 741, 742
John of Salisbury 253
Jungius, Joachim 744

Margalho, Pedro 754

Ockham, William 262, 380, 381, 382

Paul of Pergula 665
Paul of Venice 398
Peter of Spain 364, 402

Ramus, Petrus 817

Strode, Ralph 533

Thomas Aquinas 20, 500, 571, 573
Thomas of Erfurt 575

William of Sherwood 624, 625

Index of Subjects

1-633: Part One; 634-880: Part Two

Alcalá 779, 782
Ammonius: Latin 13
Analogy 305, 306, 442, 512
Arabic logic 133, 160, 187, 210, 211, 287, 454, 460, 461, 462, 463, 464, 536
Aretetic logic 85
Aristotelianism: Medieval 115, 192, 195, 200, 611
Aristotelianism: Renaissance 636, 637, 686, 819, 821, 824, 839, 841, 854
Aristotle commentary 2, 3, 5, 20, 81, 99, 100, 146, 147, 148, 149, 150, 151, 193, 196, 202, 207, 249, 288, 290, 293, 295, 296, 321, 322, 323, 328, 329, 340, 347, 386, 389, 419, 422, 423, 426, 442, 465, 491, 534, 537, 539, 541, 562, 565, 566, 570, 571, 573, 604, 627, 679, 687, 776, 825
Aristotle: Latin 19, 21, 22, 23, 24, 25, 26, 200, 342, 343, 344
Averroism 181, 829
Axiomatic method 843

Boethius commentary 209

Cambridge 480, 682, 735, 736, 737
Cicero commentary 163, 166
Combinatorics 169, 433, 434, 827, 835
Complexe significabilia 130, 155, 375, 391, 397
Composition and division 309, 485, 487, 489, 812
Connotation 314, 483, 549
Consequences 39, 44, 49, 51, 56, 82, 83, 87, 92, 188, 241, 304, 333, 337, 353, 362, 371, 402, 450, 492, 533, 554, 578, 650, 651, 663, 664, 665, 666, 730

Conversion 577
Copula 33, 34, 633
Cracow 325, 326

Definite article 33, 34
Definite description 400
Demonstration 613
Descent to singulars 595
'Dialectica' (term) 173, 339, 584
Distribution 176, 178, 466
Donatus commentary 581

England 731, 854
Existential import 119, 181, 632, 649
Exponibilia 275, 402, 652

Fallacies 152, 213, 469
Future contingents 66, 376, 380, 558, 563, 660

Germany 411, 484, 708, 723, 842
Grammar 110, 117, 244, 256, 268, 282, 414, 420, 427, 498, 504, 524, 556, 583, 723

Humanism 18, 672, 673, 703, 710, 711, 718, 723, 731, 734, 735, 736, 737, 766, 823, 824, 858, 860, 862, 865, 866, 867, 868, 871, 872, 873

Implication 9, 59, 75, 365, 643, 647, 760, 848
Induction 614
Infinite, paradox of 579
Insolubilia 59, 63, 88, 91, 93, 95, 104, 141, 142, 143, 310, 360, 402, 451, 468, 493, 514, 516, 520, 543, 545, 546, 551, 553, 564, 646, 837, 851
Intentionality 177, 355, 592, 656, 658

Intentions 16, 135, 136, 137, 211, 236, 269, 425, 429, 559, 740
Italy 140, 174, 602, 607, 680, 681, 688, 710, 718, 829, 841, 867

Language 15, 18, 126, 128, 129, 156, 157, 201, 204, 215, 216, 247, 255, 256, 257, 272, 320, 374, 404, 408, 411, 413, 417, 421, 427, 457, 459, 499, 502, 508, 513, 591, 610, 674, 748
Law 183
Logic, concept of 40, 435, 445, 529, 631, 670, 720, 767, 770, 774
Logic, history of 12, 60, 61, 62, 76, 118, 183, 195, 232, 267, 312, 325, 327, 356, 357, 361, 366, 369, 417, 421, 438, 440, 441, 443, 445, 467, 474, 509, 648, 655, 657, 733, 757, 830, 849, 853
'Logica' (term) 339
Lullism 834, 835

Manuscript sources 140, 150, 158, 159, 288, 290, 294, 295, 296, 324, 326, 328, 329, 349, 350, 480, 482, 507, 550, 551, 607, 619, 749, 750
Mathematics 713, 714, 715, 716, 808, 827, 843
Meaning 41, 126, 127, 156, 212, 272, 325, 415, 423, 431, 446, 456, 474, 525, 656, 658
Mental language 593
Method 678, 680, 681, 697, 698, 700, 717, 738, 818, 820, 828, 870, 871, 878
Modal logic 55, 57, 58, 138, 221, 264, 304, 341, 449, 486, 488, 500, 544
Modi significandi 102, 170, 191, 238, 280, 286, 331, 387, 388, 406, 501, 503, 507, 512, 556, 732, 743

Negative terms 235
Nominalism 15, 257, 271, 324, 484, 708, 719, 769

Obligations 97, 206, 213, 477, 635
Opposition 392, 773
Oxford 140, 244, 616, 617, 618, 619, 620, 682, 705, 746, 841, 850

Padua 124, 686, 698, 716, 809, 814, 818, 819, 820, 821, 844
Paralogisms 29, 153, 171
Paris 182, 620, 701, 780, 822, 823, 874, 875
Paronymy 220, 221, 227, 258
Poland 324, 327
Pons asinorum 214, 852
Porphyry commentary 1, 4, 262, 379, 418, 539
Porphyry: Latin 23
Predication 16, 588, 590, 603
Printed sources 654, 679, 693, 725, 750, 778, 784, 802, 825, 831, 842
Priscian commentary 80, 164, 203, 242, 243, 245, 251, 261, 581
Propositional logic 73, 86, 116, 145, 299, 300, 338, 367, 521, 530, 536, 544, 642, 761
Propositions 205, 274, 375, 525, 542

Ramism 691, 800, 804
Reference 41, 176, 400, 415, 656, 658
Relations 315, 316, 317, 641, 661, 662, 845
Relative terms 268, 535
Rhetoric 163, 165, 167, 173, 307, 370, 386, 491, 699, 709, 711, 731, 758, 799, 813, 832, 857, 859, 871

Salamanca 762, 765, 766, 772, 777
Significate of the proposition 43, 274, 313, 375, 409, 479, 527, 531, 596, 599
Signification 14, 70, 269, 314, 430, 458, 473, 495, 517, 724, 815
Simplicius: Latin 541
Sophisms 89, 90, 104, 182, 197, 213, 355, 407, 416, 477, 505, 506, 510, 626
Spain 675, 784, 790, 791, 792
Speculative grammar 106, 107, 108, 109, 125, 156, 186, 191, 198, 201, 204, 259, 285, 408, 428, 498, 499, 503, 509, 524, 557, 574, 575, 594, 838
Supposition 10, 27, 33, 34, 71, 78, 98, 101, 103, 139, 176, 178, 180, 225, 226, 246, 269, 334, 335, 397, 398, 399, 436, 447, 466, 470, 471, 473, 476, 494, 496, 518, 532, 548, 552,

560, 561, 576, 586, 606, 608, 644, 653, 666, 815
Syllogistic 59, 205, 234, 235, 240, 270, 340, 371, 412, 463, 611, 645, 695, 747, 843
Syncategoremata 131, 384, 402, 625

Terms 382, 397, 517, 525, 549, 796
Themistius: Latin 385

Theology 29, 117, 171, 215, 216, 237, 238, 239, 255, 320, 363, 421
Time 464, 497
Topics 48, 49, 50, 51, 52, 208, 412
Truth 69, 71, 129, 302, 310, 353, 375, 453, 458, 572, 596, 599

Universals 42, 114, 168, 199, 271, 394, 436, 561, 590, 599, 622

MAY 2 3 1989